Spelling Rules!

Janelle Ho and
Helen Pearson

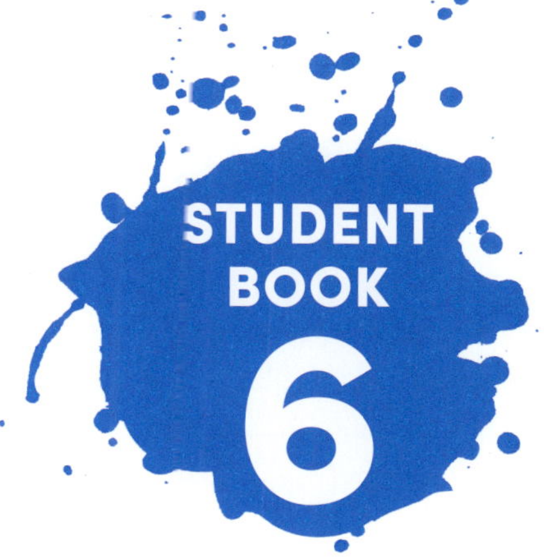

Australian Curriculum Edition

Name: ______________________________

Class: ______________________________

Contents

SLLURP

SLLURP summarises the spelling strategies that you can use to learn new words.

Say	Say the word carefully and slowly to yourself.
Listen	Listen to how each part of the word sounds in sequence.
Look	Look at the patterns of letters in the word and the shape of the word.
Understand	Understand rules, word meanings and word origins.
Remember	Remember all the similar words you can already spell and relate this knowledge to any new word.
Practise	Practise writing the word until it is firmly fixed in your long-term memory.

Scope and Sequence

	SKILL FOCUS					
UNIT	Letter patterns	Morphology	Etymology	Homophones/ Confusing words	Topic words	WORD LIST
1	ge, gi, gy, dge, j					genre, geometry, genealogy, gyrate, indulge, grudge, judgement, jubilant, jest, juvenile, junction, hijack, prejudice, adjacent, adjoining
2		-ion: adding to silent e, ve, lve, be				corruption, exhibition, exception, restriction, distinction, desperation, cooperation, alliteration, devastation, hallucination, deception, evolution, resolution, revolution, prescription
3		-ion: adding to ss, nd, de, t				possession, obsession, extension, suspension, expansion, corrosion, invasion, exclusion, collision, persuasion, provision, admission, submission, inversion, diversion
4	words ending in a vowel sound					flee, pursue, statue, venue, cocoa, mosquito, rodeo, eerie, simile, guarantee, refugee, committee, verandah, debut, alibi
5		suffixes		homographs: premier, cabinet, minister	government	government, parliament, cabinet, politician, minister, senator, representatives, governor, premier, opposition, president, election, democracy, monarchy, federal
6	REVISION					
7		syn-, sym-, co-, com-, con-, cor-, col-	*me* (dimension, immense, diameter, perimeter, thermometer, semester)			synthesise, idiosyncrasy, syndrome, sympathy, symbiotic, symmetry, coherent, cohesive, coincidence, coordinate, accommodate, commotion, compensate, correlate, collaborate
8			*optos, athlon, medeor*	homograph: coach	occupations	coach, pilot, lifeguard, locksmith, optician, treasurer, choreographer, courier, tutor, sculptor, surgeon, analyst, pharmacist, athlete, paramedic
9		-ity: adding to able, ible				stability, durability, probability, acceptability, compatibility, predictability, variability, changeability, irritability, visibility, flexibility, vulnerability, accessibility, invincibility, eligibility
10		affixes: -logy			environment	environment, rainforest, pollution, greenhouse, climate, recycle, ozone, ecology, irrigation, conservation, deforestation, flora, fauna, sustainable, atmosphere
11		bio-, zoo-, anthropo-, geo-, -graphy	*terra*			biology, biography, autobiography, biodegradable, microbe, zoology, zoophobia, anthropology, philanthropy, anthropomorphism, geology, geography, terrace, terrain, terrestrial
12	REVISION					
13	ior, ian, iar	-ity	*sen*			prior, senior, superior, exterior, posterior, deteriorate, median, alliance, valiant, pliant, ruffian, peculiar, plagiarise, matriarch, diarrhoea
14			*spek, sequi*			telescope, periscope, aspect, suspect, auspicious, conspicuous, despise, despicable, spectacle, speculate, sequence, sequel, execute, prosecute, consecutive
15		-ous				wondrous, humorous, perilous, miraculous, Indigenous, cantankerous, studious, gregarious, rebellious, voracious, precarious, instantaneous, spontaneous, righteous, ambiguous
16			*nova, vox, notare, reminisci*			novel, novelty, novice, innovate, innovation, vocal, vocabulary, advocate, vociferous, invoke, provoke, notice, notify, annotate, reminisce
17		-ic			science	solution, toxic, method, experiment, acid, alkaline, temperature, evaporate, thermometer, theory, equipment, chemical, microscope, hypothesis, laboratory
18	REVISION					
19		-ation, -ition				definition, repetition, condemnation, alteration, interpretation, continuation, declaration, cancellation, inflammation, explanation, exclamation, variation, identification, notification, clarification
20	ary, ery, ory	-ary, -ery, -ory		stationery/ stationary		military, anniversary, solitary, documentary, contrary, crockery, confectionery, surgery, nursery, treachery, forgery, sensory, contradictory, category, exploratory
21		a-, ab-, ad-, ac-				anew, akin, avert, abduct, abhor, abnormal, abolish, abrupt, abuse, adhere, adolescent, adversary, accelerate, accumulate, acquit
22			*phone, onyma, patheia, magnus*			symphony, phonetic, microphone, cacophony, synonym, antonym, pseudonym, anonymous, empathy, telepathy, majesty, majority, magnify, magnificent, magnanimous
23				homographs: organ, appendix	medicine	medicine, bacteria, virus, pregnant, fracture, organ, influenza, abdomen, intestine, capsule, appendix, vaccination, immunisation, pneumonia, stethoscope
24	REVISION					
25	cy	-cy, ob-				cyclone, cynical, cyberspace, urgency, accuracy, literacy, numeracy, privacy, pregnancy, diplomacy, adequacy, delicacy, obstinacy, buoyancy, legacy
26	double consonants					territory, graffiti, suppress, pallor, assassin, apparatus, millennium, succulent, eccentric, gimmick, dilemma, pinnacle, abbreviation, etiquette, intermittent
27		sub-, suc-, suf-, sup-, sur-				subconscious, sublime, submerge, subordinate, subside, substandard, subterranean, subtle, succinct, succumb, suffocate, suppose, supplement, surreptitious, suspend
28		multiple affixes				incomprehension, unmanageable, discontinued, ignorance, invisibility, irrational, immobile, immovable, noticeably, symmetrical, unintentionally, uncritically, reversible, illegibly, predestined
29		suffixes, plurals	non-English words		money	currency, exchange, pound, euro, rupiah, baht, allowance, financial, budget, discount, subsidy, purchase, expenditure, millionaire, treasury
30	REVISION					
31	sce, sci					ascend, descend, transcend, obscene, adolescent, fluorescent, iridescent, effervescent, miscellaneous, susceptible, convalesce, scintillate, conscience, conscientious, resuscitate
32					odd-looking words	onomatopoeia, asphalt, amateur, havoc, jargon, anemone, flummox, sleuth, nuisance, naive, pizzazz, eclipse, impromptu, labyrinth, conundrum
33			non-English words			trek, snorkel, mammoth, deluxe, carnival, rampage, maestro, berserk, gruesome, cologne, abseil, souvenir, gourmet, silhouette, entrepreneur
34			*astro*		space and time	asteroid, astronaut, astronomy, comet, galaxy, meteor, orbit, dimension, futuristic, chronology, medieval, terrestrial, archaeologist, palaeontology, Renaissance
35	REVISION					

NOTE TO TEACHERS AND PARENTS

Spelling Rules!

Some students are natural spellers. But the vast majority of students need formal, systematic and sequential instruction about the way spelling works and the strategies they can use to become independent, confident spellers and spelling risk-takers.

The *Spelling Rules!* program is based on sound linguistic and pedagogical theory. It is informed by research into how students of different ages acquire and apply spelling skills, and how those skills move from the working to the long-term memory. The program closely follows the Australian English curriculum. *Australian Curriculum: English* references are provided in the Teacher Resource Books. The program consists of seven student books, fully supported by two Teacher Resource Books.

Each student book contains units of work, with each unit designed to be used over the course of a week. The content of each unit simultaneously develops new skills and reinforces skills from previous units and earlier books. The introduction of new letter patterns is logically sequenced and takes into account both frequency of use and complexity. Where appropriate, topic words from other curriculum areas such as mathematics, science and social sciences are included. When spelling rules are introduced, only known sounds and letter patterns are used so that students focus on one skill at a time. Regular revision units enable teachers to assess student progress and reinforce key rules and patterns from previous units.

Spelling knowledge

Learning to spell involves developing different kinds of spelling knowledge. In many cases, particularly in the upper grades, more than one kind of knowledge is called upon at a time. As they work through the activities in each *Spelling Rules!* unit, students will develop:

- **Kinaesthetic knowledge** – the physical feeling when saying different sounds and words, and when writing the shapes of letters and words
- **Phonological knowledge** – how a word sounds and the patterns of sounds in words
- **Visual knowledge** – how letters and words look and the visual patterns in words
- **Morphemic knowledge** – the meaning or function of words or parts of words
- **Etymological knowledge** – the origins and history of words and the effect this has on spelling patterns.

Icons used in Student Book 6

This icon highlights useful spelling rules. The rule is always introduced the first time students will need it to complete an activity. There is also a handy summary of important rules on page 80.

This icon tells students that a special clue or hint is provided for an activity. It may be a spelling, grammar or punctuation convention, or a definition of a useful term.

Spelling Rules! Student Book 6 (ISBN 9780655092728) © Janelle Ho, Helen Pearson

Student Book 6

Units of work

Student Book 6 contains 35 weekly units of work. See the **Scope and Sequence chart** on page 3 for more information. Each revision unit gives students an opportunity to self-assess.

Word lists

In *Student Book 6* each unit (except Revision) has a list of spelling words. The core words in the lists have been chosen to support the learning focus and strategies being taught in the unit.

Spelling lists enable a spelling element to be focused on, and provide sufficient examples to consolidate the teaching point. Topic words come from other curriculum areas, such as mathematics and social sciences. In addition, homophones and words that are easily confused with each other are explained and practised.

SLLURP

Each word list begins with a reminder for students to SLLURP. SLLURP summarises the strategies that will help spelling move from students' working memory to their long-term memory. These strategies are provided on page 2, for easy reference.

Unit at a glance

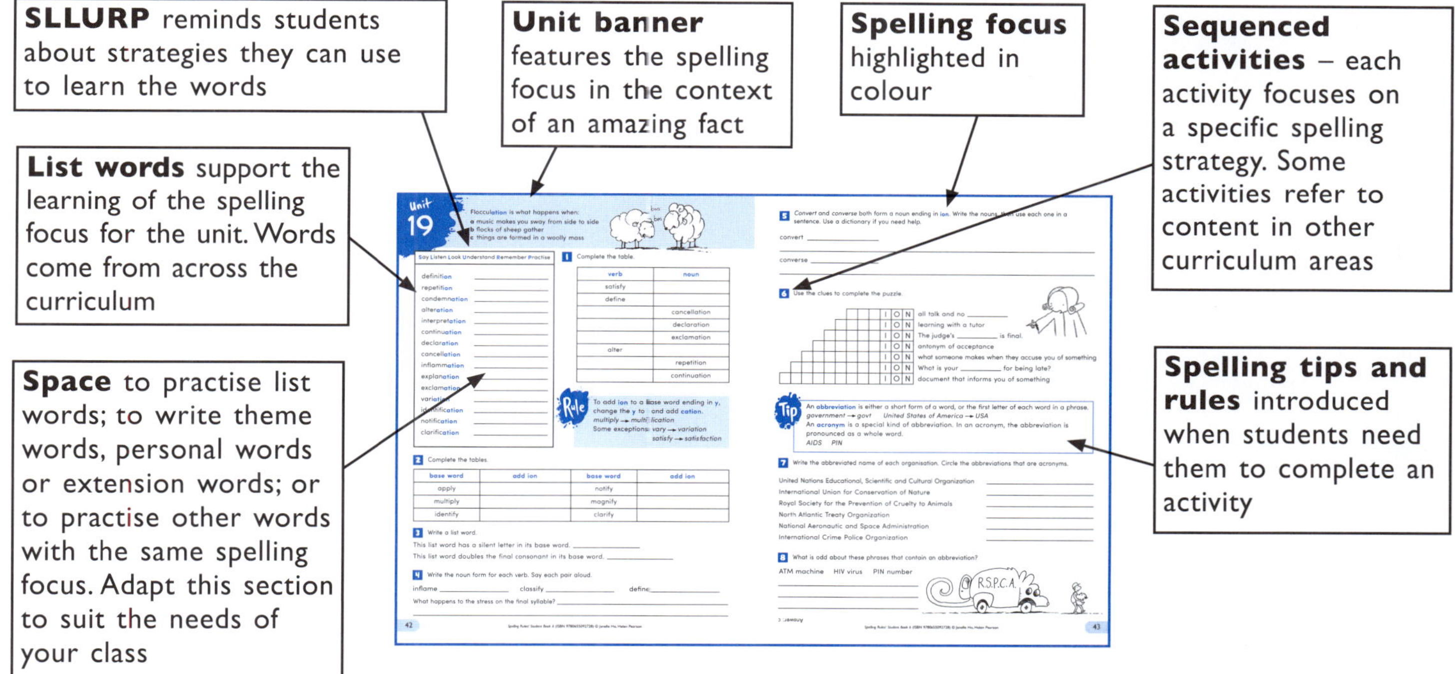

Spelling Rules! Teacher Resource Book 3–6

Full teacher support for *Student Book 6* is provided by *Spelling Rules! Teacher Resource Book 3–6*. Here you will find valuable background information about spelling development and spelling knowledge, along with practical resources, such as:

- teaching tips for every unit in *Student Book 6*
- extra word lists
- strategies for teaching spelling
- guidelines for assessment and diagnosis of errors
- activities to support struggling spellers
- worthwhile extension for more able spellers.

Unit 1

Julienne describes:

a the naming of a baby girl
b something cut into thin strips
c plans for a party in July

Say Listen Look Understand Remember Practise

genre	______
geometry	______
genealogy	______
gyrate	______
indulge	______
grudge	______
judgement	______
jubilant	______
jest	______
juvenile	______
junction	______
hijack	______
prejudice	______
adjacent	______
adjoining	______

Tip **g** usually has a soft sound when it is followed by **e**, **i** or **y**.

1 Circle the letter **g** if it has a soft sound.

gentle	energy	goalpost
gigantic	gymnasium	genius
ginger	gear	gallop
grudge	genealogy	giddy

2 Use some of the letters in each word to make new words with a hard **g** sound.

passenger ______
urgent ______
gyrate ______
pledge ______
genre ______
geometry ______

Tip Prefixes and suffixes are known as **affixes**.

3 Break each word into its base word and affix.

geometric = ______ + ______
adjoining = ______ + ______ + ______
jester = ______ + ______
disadvantage = ______ + ______

4 Use the list words as verbs, nouns and adjectives. You may need to add or delete an affix. Try not to use the same word more than once.

verbs	nouns	adjectives
to ______ a plane	the book's ______	a ______ champ
to ______ wildly	a traffic ______	an ______ room
to ______ in dessert	to hold a ______	a ______ pattern
to ______ harshly	treated with ______	a ______ animal

5 Write two list words that are synonyms. ____________ ____________

6 Complete the passage with words beginning with **j**.

In the Australian ____________ system, anybody accused of a crime is defended by a lawyer. In court, there is a ____________, who knows the law and controls what happens in the courtroom. A group of ordinary people called the ____________ makes the final decision about whether the defendant is guilty. If not guilty, the accused is free to leave. If guilty, the judge makes a ____________ about an appropriate punishment.

7 Write words with a **j** or soft **g** sound. The first letter is given.

The contents of the box are f____________. Please carry it carefully.

Mum made an a____________ to the length of my pyjamas so my little brother could wear them.

I am of a____________ height, but my sister is tall for her age.

Karl longed to travel as a p____________ on the Trans-Siberian railway.

My father has a cat a____________. They make him sneeze.

I issued a c____________ to replay the game because I wanted r____________.

Dad tells us that holding a g____________ can make one ill.

My grandparents tested their g____________ and found that they have Dutch ancestors!

8 Which genre of books do you most like to read? Write a paragraph explaining why.

____

____

____

____

____

____

____

____

____

____

____

____

Answer: b

Unit 2

Fluctuation occurs when:

a fruit becomes rotten
b a flock of ducks flies in formation
c something changes constantly

Say Listen Look Understand Remember Practise

corruption	____
exhibition	____
exception	____
restriction	____
distinction	____
desperation	____
cooperation	____
alliteration	____
devastation	____
hallucination	____
deception	____
evolution	____
resolution	____
revolution	____
prescription	____

1 Write the two list words that are different by only one letter.

____ ____

2 Complete the table.

verb	noun
attract	
	injection
	detection
exhibit	
exhaust	
	digestion
reject	
	direction
	infection
inspect	

Rule If the verb ends in silent **e**, drop the **e** before adding **ion**. *devote → devotion*

3 Write the noun form.

alliterate ____ separate ____ pollute ____ cooperate ____

4 Write the base word.

education ____ irrigation ____ hallucination ____

desperation ____ appreciation ____ devastation ____

Spelling Rules! Student Book 6 (ISBN 9780655092728) © Janelle Ho, Helen Pearson

If a word ends in **lve**, change **ve** to **ut** before adding **ion**.
dissolve → dissolution

5 Make a noun by adding **ion**.

evolve ______ resolve ______ solve ______ revolve ______

If the base word includes **scribe**, change **scribe** to **script** before adding **ion**.
describe → description

6 Complete the table. All the words follow the same pattern.

verb	noun
prescribe	
subscribe	
inscribe	
transcribe	

If the base word has the word element **ceive**, change **ceive** to **cept** before adding **ion**.
receive → reception

7 Complete the table. All the words follow the same pattern.

verb	noun
deceive	
	perception
	conception

8 Use the clue to make a new word that matches the definition.

word	clue	new word	definition
detection	change a letter	______	gloominess
distinction	change 1st syllable	______	end of a species
digestion	change 1st syllable	______	build-up of traffic
revolution	change a letter	______	conclusion

Answer: c

Unit 3

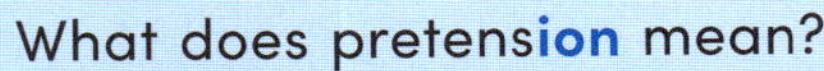

What does pretens**ion** mean?

a a claim that you deserve merit when you don't
b a number before ten
c preparing tent ropes

Say **L**isten **L**ook **U**nderstand **R**emember **P**ractise

possess**ion** ______
obsess**ion** ______
extens**ion** ______
suspens**ion** ______
expans**ion** ______
corros**ion** ______
invas**ion** ______
exclus**ion** ______
collis**ion** ______
persuas**ion** ______
provis**ion** ______
admiss**ion** ______
submiss**ion** ______
invers**ion** ______
divers**ion** ______

Rule Some verbs add **ion** to make the noun.

1 Write the noun.

possess	impress
______	______
confess	discuss
______	______
concuss	obsess
______	______

impress...

2 Describe the pattern used in question 1.

______
______

Rule For some words ending in **t**, change **t** to **ss** before adding **ion**.

admit → admission

If a word ends in **nd**, change **d** to **s** before adding **ion**.

extend → extension

3 Write the noun.

permit ______ submit ______ omit ______
expand ______ suspend ______ comprehend ______

4 *Admit* has two related nouns: *admission* and *admittance*. Use a dictionary to find the meaning of each word. Use each word in a sentence.

admission ______
______

admittance ______
______

Spelling Rules! Student Book 6 (ISBN 9780655092728) © Janelle Ho, Helen Pearson

If the verb ends in **de**, drop the **e** and change **d** to **s** before adding **ion**.
divide → division

5 Write the noun form.

explode	collide	invade	exclude	persuade
______	______	______	______	______
conclude	include	erode	decide	evade
______	______	______	______	______

Tip

Some words are always used together. This is called **collocation**.
separation from not *separation with*
The underlined words are **prepositions**.

6 Write a list word and the preposition it goes with to complete each sentence.

The player's ______________ ______ the first team was due to injury.

The ______________ ______ the project deadline was greeted with cheers by the whole class.

Susie didn't have to say anything; her face was an ______________ ______ her guilt.

The shattered glass at the intersection was due to the ______________ ______ two cars earlier.

Mr King displays his ______________ ______ toy cars in his shed. It's full to the ceiling!

There was rust on the machine due to ______________ ______ the iron parts.

7 Rewrite each sentence using a list word. If you can, begin your sentence with the list word.

The scientist Charles Darwin proposed a theory of how living things have evolved.

____

This year I have resolved to talk to one new person a month.

____

The local council has finally said they will permit my parents to build a pool!

____

My prize-winning painting will be exhibited in the Town Hall next month.

____

Anyone caught writing graffiti on the walls will be suspended.

____

Answer: a

Unit 4

What is whang**ee**?

a the opposite of a wedgie
b bamboo used for making canes
c someone who has made one hundred bungee jumps

Say **L**isten **L**ook **U**nderstand **R**emember **P**ractise

flee ____________
pursue ____________
statue ____________
venue ____________
cocoa ____________
mosquito ____________
rodeo ____________
eerie ____________
simile ____________
guarantee ____________
refugee ____________
committee ____________
verandah ____________
debut ____________
alibi ____________

1 Write list words that end with these sounds.

long o as in toe ____________ ____________ ____________

long e as in key ____________ ____________ ____________ ____________ ____________ ____________

long oo as in true ____________ ____________ ____________ ____________

2 Write a list word that has a silent letter.

____

3 Which list word is a homophone? Write each word and its meaning.

____________ ____________________
____________ ____________________

4 Write the plural.

verandah	mosquito	refugee	volcano	alibi
____________	____________	____________	____________	____________

5 Write the language each word comes from and its meaning. Use a dictionary if you need help.

	language	**meaning**
cocoa	____________	____________________
rodeo	____________	____________________
verandah	____________	____________________
debut	____________	____________________
alibi	____________	____________________

Spelling Rules! Student Book 6 (ISBN 9780655092728) © Janelle Ho, Helen Pearson

6 Most of the vowels have been left out of these sentences. Write each sentence correctly.

Ths nw cmptr gdgt cms wth a fr-yr grnte.

____

Th wnd whstlng thrgh th crck in th wndw mks n eri snd.

____

Do y knw th vnu fr th drss rhrsl?

____

Lins prsu thr pry in pcks t incrs thr chncs of mkng a kll.

____

Tip

A **simile** describes something by comparing it to something else.
It uses *like* or *as* to make the comparison.
The dancer flopped around like a fish out of water.
The dancer moved as gracefully as a swan.

7 Write similes using these words.

statue ______________________________

cocoa ______________________________

eerie ______________________________

rodeo ______________________________

mosquito ______________________________

8 Write list words.

The local community hall will be a good ____________ for our meeting.

Hot ____________ can warm you up in winter.

The ____________ net around my bed has a hole in it, and I got bitten last night.

The light before the thunderstorm was ____________.

9 Write the correct form of the verb to complete each sentence.

The police ____________ the shoplifters and eventually caught them.
pursue

This gold pass ____________ you free entry to the movies for one year!
guarantee

Our cat Mimi ____________ into the house when the dogs started barking.
flee

Answer: b

Unit 5

A di**archy** is:
a two arches in a row
b a human with two heads
c a State governed by two rulers

Say Listen Look Understand Remember Practise

government ______
parliament ______
cabinet ______
politician ______
minister ______
senator ______
representatives ______
governor ______
premier ______
opposition ______
president ______
election ______
democracy ______
monarchy ______
federal ______

1 Break each word into its base word and suffix.

government = ______ + ______
election = ______ + ______
monarchy = ______ + ______
opposition = ______ + ______
politician = ______ + ______
president = ______ + ______
governor = ______ + ______

2 Look at the words in question 1.

Which words have the same base word?

______ ______

In which words does the base word change when the suffix is added?

______ ______
______ ______

3 Write the list words that refer to people who work in government. Circle the word that is not a member of the Australian government.

______ ______ ______ ______
______ ______ ______

4 Many abbreviations are used in government. What do these abbreviations stand for?

PM ______ MHR ______
MP ______ GG ______

5 Write commonly used abbreviations for these words.

federal ______ government ______ representatives ______

Spelling Rules! Student Book 6 (ISBN 9780655092728) © Janelle Ho, Helen Pearson

6 Look up each word in a dictionary. Write a definition and the language each one comes from.

monarchy ______________________________

____

democracy ______________________________

____

Tip A word that is spelt the same as another but has a different meaning is called a **homograph**. The noun *bear*, meaning *a big furry mammal*, is a homograph of the verb *bear*, meaning *to endure* or *to carry*.

7 These words are **homographs**. Think of two different meanings for each word. Write a sentence to show each meaning.

premier: 1. ______________________________
2. ______________________________

cabinet: 1. ______________________________
2. ______________________________

minister: 1. ______________________________
2. ______________________________

8 Add **affixes** to the base word to form related words.

depend ______________________________

democrat ______________________________

oppose ______________________________

federal ______________________________

elect ______________________________

9 Write the correct form of list words to complete the passage.

Most countries are ____________. In these countries, the citizens ____________ their government. In one type of democracy, such as in Australia and Singapore, the government is headed by a prime ____________. In another type of democracy, such as in the United States and France, the government is headed by a ____________. The role of the ____________ is to question government decisions and propose alternative policies.

Answer: c

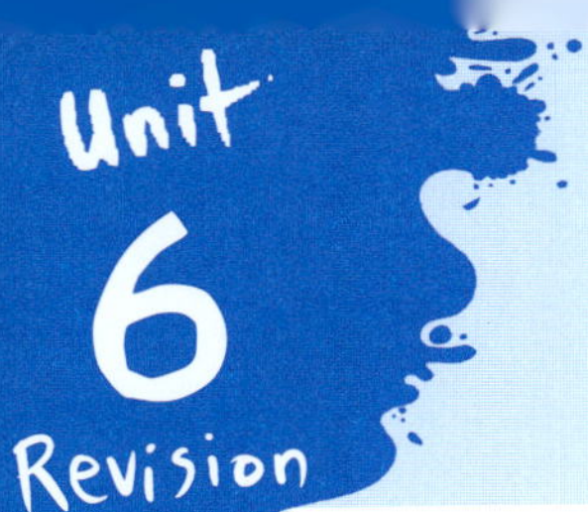

What is your problem if you are suffering from verbiage?
a you are constantly making up new verbs
b you are allergic to the smell of rotting vegetables
c you use many redundant words

persuade
oppose
pursue

1 Complete the table.

verb	add ed	add ing	noun
persuade	persuaded		
exhibit			exhibition
digest			digestion
admit		admitting	
decide	decided		
guarantee	guaranteed		
invert		inverting	

2 Write double letters to complete each word.

a __ __ociation o __ __osition pa __ __enger permi __ __ion cha __ __enge
c __ __peration co __ __i __ __ __ __ __ __rie a __ __reciation admi __ __ion

3 Write g or j.

pre __udice ad __acent refu __ee ur __ent fra __ile jud __e

4 Write the missing letter or letters that make the s or sh sound.

rejoi __e appre __ia __ __on adju __tment exten __ __on
revolu __ __on prejudi __e exhibi __ __on justi __e
democra __y expan __ __on

5 Rearrange the letters to make an appropriate word.

I received a tintiondisc in the competition. __________
As time ran out, the teams played with increasing spontraidee. __________
Japan has the oldest chomanyr in the world. __________
I'm good at basketball but only gaverea in swimming. __________
Granddad has to go to the doctor to renew his pitcrosprine. __________
When the weather is cool, we like to sit out on the rahdenva. __________

Spelling Rules! Student Book 6 (ISBN 9780655092728) © Janelle Ho, Helen Pearson

6 Use the clues to complete the puzzle.

									1.		E
								2.			E
							3.	E			
						4.			E		
					5.					E	
				6.					E		
			7.	E							
		8.				E					
	9.					E					

1. enemy
2. run away from
3. first public appearance
4. needed immediately
5. group of senior government ministers
6. next to
7. Darwin's theory of ___________
8. something that is owned
9. working well together

7 Add a suitable prefix.

_____digestion   _____advantage   _____justice   _____decision   _____judge

8 Proofread this text. The text has six words that are incorrect. Circle the mistakes. Then write the correct spelling of the words in the boxes.

I knew the little cakes on the bench were for morning tea and I would never get permition to have one now. Maybe the solussion was to sneak a couple while no one was around, and avoid detecsion. I had one in my hand when Dad came into the kitchen, so I stuffed it in my mouth. Eating that quickly is bad for the digeston! I've made a resolusion not to do it again, because it's worse than making an admition with your mouth full!

9 Use the anagram to write a list word that matches the definition.

anagram	word	definition
car comedy	____________	government by the people
green	____________	text type
jab until	____________	extremely joyful
toenail trail	____________	device where words begin with the same sound
moo quits	____________	an insect with an itchy bite
bean tic	____________	furniture to display items
cool is nil	____________	crash
red leaf	____________	government where power is shared with the states
so drive in	____________	distraction

Answer: c

Unit 7

Which shape is **sym**metrical?

a 

b 

c

Say Listen Look Understand Remember Practise	
synthesise	______________
idio**syn**crasy	______________
syndrome	______________
sympathy	______________
symbiotic	______________
symmetry	______________
coherent	______________
cohesive	______________
coincidence	______________
coordinate	______________
ac**com**modate	______________
commotion	______________
compensate	______________
correlate	______________
collaborate	______________

Tip

The unstressed vowel sound is called a **schwa**. This sound can be written in many ways.

away *animal* *literal* *bitten* *action* *kingdom* *evil*

1 For each list word, underline the letters that make the **schwa**. Not every word contains a schwa.

synthesise	idiosyncrasy	syndrome
sympathy	symbiotic	symmetry
coherent	cohesive	coincidence
coordinate	accommodate	commotion
compensate	correlate	collaborate

2 Write your name and underline the **schwa** if there is one.

____

Tip

com- and **syn-** mean *with* or *together*. **com-** is Latin in origin and **syn-** is Greek in origin.

3 Use a dictionary to write the word origins. Then answer the question.

syndrome: syn (together) + ______________ = a set of symptoms that go together to indicate a disease

sympathy: sym (together) + ______________ = the sharing of another person's emotions

symbiotic: sym (together) + ______________ = dependent on each other; living together

symmetry: sym (together) + ______________ = where one side is the same as the other

When does **syn-** change to **sym-**?

____

Use **com-** before **b**, **p** or **m**. Use **col-** before **l**. Use **cor-** before **r**.
Use **co-** before **h** or **gn**. Use **con-** in all other cases.

4 Write **com**, **col**, **cor**, **co** or **con** to finish each word.

_____lect	re_____gnise	_____cave	_____pany
_____dolence	_____herent	_____pliment	_____ment
_____bine	_____respond	_____league	_____fident

5 Write two list words that mean *work together*. ____________________ ____________________

6 Use list words to complete the puzzle.

7 Write a list word that matches the definition.

____________________ behaviour unique to a person

____________________ housing; a place to live

____________________ disturbance; noise

____________________ events happening together

Answer: b

Unit 8

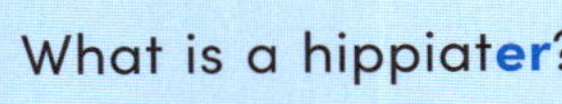

What is a hippiater?

a a hip surgeon
b a species of alligator
c a horse doctor

Say Listen Look Understand Remember Practise

coach ______
pilot ______
lifeguard ______
locksmith ______
optician ______
treasurer ______
choreographer ______
courier ______
tutor ______
sculptor ______
surgeon ______
analyst ______
pharmacist ______
athlete ______
paramedic ______

1 Complete the table.

occupation	base word
engineer	
treasurer	
	law
	account
	pharmacy
scientist	
analyst	
translator	
	politic

2 Write the two list words that are also compound words.

______ ______

3 Write a list word that fits each group.

nurse anaesthetist doctor ______

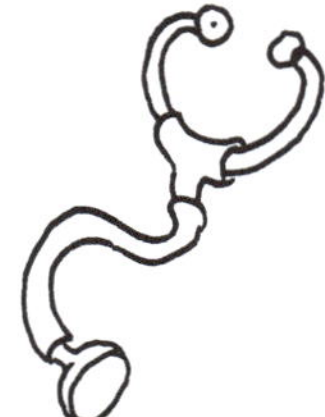

artist painter illustrator ______

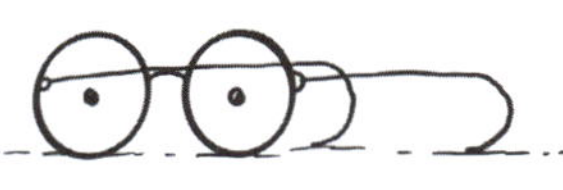

optometrist ophthalmologist ______

teacher lecturer professor ______

4 Write the occupation of a person who works in each place.

laboratory ______
restaurant ______
beach ______
aeroplane ______
ambulance ______
art studio ______

Spelling Rules! Student Book 6 (ISBN 9780655092728) © Janelle Ho, Helen Pearson

5 *Optos* is Greek for *seen, visible*; *opsis* means *a sight*. Write the meanings of the related words. Underline the part of the word that comes from *optos* or *opsis*.

optician ____________________

optical ____________________

synopsis ____________________

autopsy ____________________

6 Use a dictionary to write the meanings of the root words. What language is the root word in?

athlon ____________________

medeor ____________________

7 Write a word to match the definition. The root word is given.

an event consisting of ten challenges (*athlon*) ____________

the science of restoring or maintaining health (*medeor*) ____________

someone trained to help a doctor as part of a rescue team (*medeor*) ____________

8 Add **er**, **eer**, **or**, **ian** or **ist** to complete these occupation names. Use a dictionary if you need help.

design____	anaesthet____	music____
curat____	carpent____	zoolog____
mountain____	guitar____	librar____
edit____	electric____	invent____
ornitholog____	plumb____	engine____

9 The text has six words that are incorrect. Circle the mistakes. Then write the correct spelling of the words in the boxes.

I enjoy watching the Olympic Games. The venu is usually colourful, with the many flags of the participating nations. The atheletes exibit great skill and courage as they persue their dreams and the crowds cheer their appresiation. I feel I am always guranteed great entertainment.

10 *Coach* can be both a noun and a verb. Write a sentence for each meaning of the word.

coach (noun): ____________________

____

coach (verb): ____________________

____

Answer: c

Unit 9

Risibility is the ability to:

a rise early
b laugh easily
c rotate your wrists

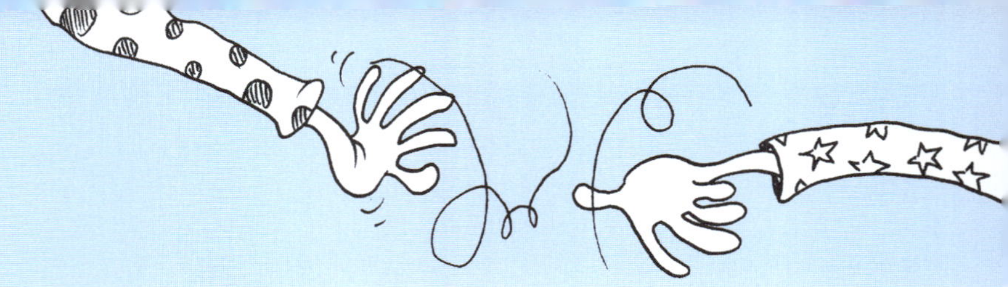

Say Listen Look Understand Remember Practise

stabil**ity**	______
durabil**ity**	______
probabil**ity**	______
acceptabil**ity**	______
compatibil**ity**	______
predictabil**ity**	______
variabil**ity**	______
changeabil**ity**	______
irritabil**ity**	______
visibil**ity**	______
flexibil**ity**	______
vulnerabil**ity**	______
accessibil**ity**	______
invincibil**ity**	______
eligibil**ity**	______

Words ending in **ible** and **able** are adjectives. These words may also add **ity** as a second suffix.
Adding **ity** changes the adjective to a noun.

1 Write the list words ending in **ibility**. Then write the adjectival form.

noun	adjective

2 Write the list words ending in **ability**. Then write the adjectival form.

noun	adjective

noun	adjective

3 Write the list word in which silent **e** has been kept when the suffixes are added to the base word.

______

Another word that keeps silent **e** is *traceability*. Why do these words keep the silent **e**?

______

4 Use each clue to find a smaller word within a list word. Write the small word and the list word.

clue	answer	list word
the opposite of *out*	______	______
what thieves do	______	______
the colour of anger or embarrassment	______	______
what you do to show off your muscles	______	______
tap gently with affection	______	______

5 Add **un**, **im**, **in** or **ir** to make an antonym.

____flexibility	____probability	____predictability	____responsibility
____reliability	____ability	____stability	____compatibility
____eligibility	____regularity	____visibility	____likeability

6 Write a list word that ends in **ibility** or **ability**.

Cyber criminals look for a ______________ so they can hack into the system.

Lili avoids ______________ and constantly surprises us with new magic tricks.

Our bushwalk was cancelled due to the ______________ of a thunderstorm.

Buster, our dog, has been bad-tempered recently. Our vet discovered that his ______________ was due to an ear infection.

The ______________ criteria for the award are listed on the council website.

It is the ______________ of superheroes that we most want!

______________ to buildings is important for people with mobility problems.

7 Make a noun from each adjective. What does each noun mean?

	noun	meaning
audible	______	______
invincible	______	______
durable	______	______
feasible	______	______
manoeuvrable	______	______

Answer: b

Unit 10

What is tricho**logy**?

a the science of hair and its diseases
b the knowledge of three-sided objects
c the study of tricks

Say Listen Look Understand Remember Practise

environment ______
rainforest ______
pollution ______
greenhouse ______
climate ______
recycle ______
ozone ______
ecology ______
irrigation ______
conservation ______
deforestation ______
flora ______
fauna ______
sustainable ______
atmosphere ______

1 Write the affixes used in the list words.

suffixes ______ ______
______ ______

prefixes ______
______

2 Write the base words.

pollution ______
irrigation ______
conservation ______
sustainable ______
recycle ______
emission ______

3 Write the list words that are compound words.

______ ______

Tip

Prefixes and suffixes (affixes) add to the meaning of a base word.
de + *forest* + *ation* = the process of getting rid of forests

4 Write the meanings of these words. Use a dictionary if you need help.

reforestation ______
unsustainable ______
pollutants ______

5 Use each clue to find a smaller word within a list word. Write the small word and the list word.

clue	answer	list word
a 3D shape	______	______
a number	______	______
a discoloured patch	______	______
where a train stops	______	______

6 Use some of the letters in each list word to make a three-letter, a four-letter and a five-letter word.

	environment	**irrigation**	**sustainable**
3 letters	______	______	______
4 letters	______	______	______
5 letters	______	______	______

7 Use list words to complete the diagram. Briefly explain the diagram.

______ + ______ → the ______ effect → ______ change and rising sea levels

______

______

______

Tip **logy** is a word element that means *science* or *the study of.*
bio (living things) + *logy* → *biology*

8 Use a dictionary to find the meaning of each word. Write the meaning, then use the word in a sentence.

ecology ______

______

psychology ______

______

zoology ______

______

meteorology ______

______

9 Use a list word to name each category. Add more examples.

______: trees, shrubs, grass, ______, ______

______: mammals, insects, fish, ______, ______

______: hose, dam, water pipe, ______, ______

Answer: a

Unit 11

Terra means *earth* or *land*.

What does *tetra* mean?

a test
b shape
c four

Say **L**isten **L**ook **U**nderstand **R**emember **P**ractise

biology ______
biography ______
autobiography ______
biodegradable ______
microbe ______
zoology ______
zoophobia ______
anthropology ______
philanthropy ______
anthropomorphism ______
geology ______
geography ______
terrace ______
terrain ______
terrestrial ______

Tip The suffixes **-logy** and **-graphy** show area of study. **-logy** means *science* or *the study of*. **-graphy** is used for art or a science that describes a subject.

1 Write **-logy** or **-graphy**.

photo______ bio______
techno______ choreo______
meteoro______ geo______
etymo______ cinemato______
oceano______ psycho______
eco______ ornitho______
genea______ palaeonto______

2 **bio-** and **geo-** can add both **-logy** and **-graphy**. Write the meanings of the words.

biology ______
biography ______
geology ______
geography ______

3 Write the meanings of each element in the word.

biodegradable = bio + de + grade + able

= ______ + ______ + ______ + ______

microbe = micro + bio

= ______ + ______

anthropomorphism = anthropo + morph + ism

= ______ + ______ + ______

Spelling Rules! Student Book 6 (ISBN 9780655092728) © Janelle Ho, Helen Pearson

Anthropomorphism is a technique in which animals or gods are given human qualities.
My cat felt sorry when I hurt myself.

4 Use anthropomorphism to write a story about animals.

____

____

____

____

____

5 Write the occupation.

biology	zoology	geology	anthropology
________	________	________	________
biography	geography	philanthropy	
________	________	________	

6 *Terra* means *earth* or *land*. Rearrange the letters to write a word that has the root word *terra*.

We went out onto the ____________ (ractree) to look at the night sky.

Our ____________ (rireret) barks if there's a full moon.

In our solar system, Venus, Mars, Mercury and Earth are ____________ (lateristerr) planets.

Australia has six states and ten ____________ (rortisetire).

The ____________ (rainter) is rocky, so walkers should take extra time.

7 The word *phobia* means *extreme fear*. What phobias can you think of?

____

____

Answer: c

Unit 12 Revision

What is a snott**er**?

a a rope attached to a ship's mast
b a person with a cold
c a sick pig

1 Write the letters that make the **schwa** sound.

clim___te desp___at___n cabin___t prej___dice biol___gy
sculpt___ couri___ opp___tun___ty coher___nt surg___n

2 Write the noun form.

disturb ____________ decide ____________
expand ____________ accept ____________
transmit ____________ translate ____________
possess ____________ govern ____________

3 Write an occupation associated with each picture.

____________ ____________
____________ ____________

4 Use a prefix to make the antonym.

permanent ____________ certainty ____________ flexibility ____________
sustainable ____________ possibility ____________ stability ____________

5 Use each word in a sentence.

invisibility ____
invincibility ____

6 Colour the correct word.

Fireworks have a terrible | affect | effect | on my dog, who howls and whimpers.

Dad's taking me to buy some | stationary | stationery | for my project.

I had to | practice | practise | for weeks before I could hold my | breath | breathe | long enough to swim across the pool underwater.

The charity shop | accepts | excepts | all donations | accept | except | furniture.

Spelling Rules! Student Book 6 (ISBN 9780655092728) © Janelle Ho, Helen Pearson

7 Rewrite each sentence using one word to replace the underlined word or phrase.

Pulling at his hair when he is nervous is his behaviour that identifies him.

Airports must close if fog reduces the ability to see.

We put our empty bottles in the yellow bin so that they can be made into something else.

The world has to be careful about getting rid of all the forests, or our way of life may not be able to be sustained.

Police were called to calm a noisy disturbance at the store.

The actor's story of her own life is eagerly anticipated.

8 Write the correct form of the verb to complete each sentence.

Our team captain later ____________ (accept) responsibility for mixing up the time of our match.

Yesterday, Alan ____________ (admit) that he used to believe in bunyips.

Everyone had to ____________ (cooperate) to complete the obstacle course.

Were you ____________ (disturb) by the thunderstorm last night?

____________ (change) my shirt at half time definitely helped me play better.

Joey ____________ (sympathy) with me when he heard my gerbil was ill.

9 Write about a job you might like to have as an adult.

Answer: a

Unit 13

What does it mean to ride pillion?

a to be a passenger on a motorcycle
b to deliver medicines in a van
c to carry pillows on a bike

Say **L**isten **L**ook **U**nderstand **R**emember **P**ractise

prior ____________
senior ____________
superior ____________
exterior ____________
posterior ____________
deteriorate ____________
median ____________
alliance ____________
valiant ____________
pliant ____________
ruffian ____________
peculiar ____________
plagiarise ____________
matriarch ____________
diarrhoea ____________

1 Write a list word that rhymes.

fire ____________
defiance ____________
giant ____________
idea ____________

2 Write the list word that is an antonym.

junior ____________
inferior ____________
disunity ____________
interior ____________
ordinary ____________

3 Write the list word that is a synonym.

union ____________
decline ____________
courageous ____________
forge ____________

Tip *Interior, exterior, posterior* and *anterior* describe different positions. The first syllable indicates the position.

4 Complete each sentence.

If *postpone* means *put off until later*, then **post** means ____________.
If *antenatal* means *before birth*, then **ante** means ____________.
If *external* means *outside*, then **ex** means ____________.
If *internal* means *inside*, then **in** means ____________.

5 Draw a line to match each word to its meaning.

interior	before
exterior	inside
anterior	behind
posterior	outside

The interior is warmer than the exterior.

Spelling Rules! Student Book 6 (ISBN 9780655092728) © Janelle Ho, Helen Pearson

A **mnemonic** helps you remember something tricky.
*Bring your **ears** to reh**ears**als.*
*There is **a rat** in sep**arat**e.*

6 Make up a mnemonic to help you remember the spelling of *diarrhoea.*

____

Tip

Many of the list words add **ity** to make the noun.
prior → *priority*

7 Add **ity** to make the noun.

prior	____________	senior	____________
inferior	____________	peculiar	____________
superior	____________	familiar	____________

8 **sen** is a root word meaning *old.* Circle the word in each pair that has that root word. Then write a sentence that uses that word.

senior	sender	____________________
sensible	senator	____________________
sensation	senile	____________________
		____________________

9 Use the clues to complete the puzzle. If there is no clue, the word is a list word. Write your own clue for that word.

		1		2 D								3 P			4	
	5									6 T						
7	A			A												
															N	
	I															
				8 O						O		A				
9	L			A												

Help!

Across

1. ____________
3. ____________
7. giving out or reflecting light
8. once in a while
9. ____________

Down

2. ____________
3. ____________
4. a point of view
5. logical
6. teaching or instruction

Answer: a

Unit 14

If a **sequel** follows the main story, what comes before the main story?

a a forequel
b a prequel
c a subquel

Say Listen Look Understand Remember Practise	
telescope	________
periscope	________
aspect	________
suspect	________
auspicious	________
conspicuous	________
despise	________
despicable	________
spectacle	________
speculate	________
sequence	________
sequel	________
execute	________
prosecute	________
consecutive	________

Tip Etymology is the study of the origin of words.

Tip *spek* is a root word that means *to observe*. It is found in the Latin word *scopium* and in the Greek word *skopein*, which mean *to look at* or *examine*.

1 Write the list words that have *skopein* in their etymology.

____

____

2 **-scope** is used to indicate a viewing instrument. Write the meanings of the other word parts.

telescope: an instrument that makes distant objects appear closer

tele: ________

periscope: an instrument for viewing objects that are not in direct sight

peri: ________

Tip *spek* is also found in the Latin word *specere*, which means *to look*.

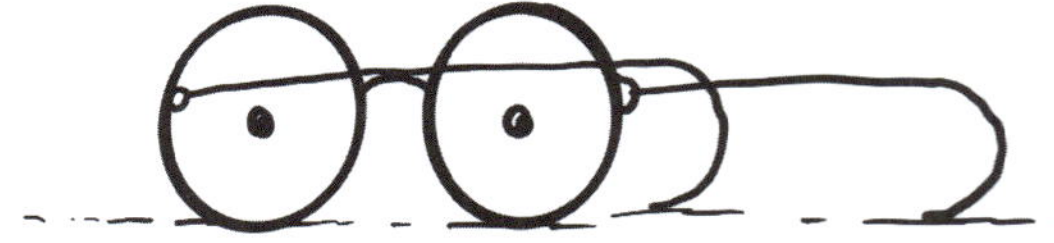

3 Write the list words that have *specere* in their etymology. You may consult your dictionary.

________ ________ ________ ________

________ ________ ________ ________

4 Add an affix to make a word from the same word family. Make sure your word is from a different grammatical class.

despise ________________ auspicious ________________

spectacular ________________ suspect ________________

execute ________________ consecutive ________________

Tip *sequi* is a Latin word that means *to follow*.

5 Write the list words that have *sequi* in their etymology.

________________ ________________ ________________

________________ ________________

6 *sequel*, *sequence* and *consecutive* are closely related in meaning. Use each word in a sentence. Can you write a short text using all three words?

____

____

____

7 A malapropism is an inaccurate use of similar sounding words. Circle the malapropism in each sentence and write the correct word.

Our teacher asked us to spectacle on what will happen next in the story. ________________

The police plan to execute the criminal on charges of identity theft. ________________

Grace is so tall that she is conscientious wherever she goes. ________________

The consecutive of the injury was that the team had to play without their captain. ________________

Smashing the windows of the care home is disposable! ________________

Tip Some nouns appear only in the plural form. *spectacles* *trousers* *scissors*

8 Write a plural-only noun to complete each sentence.

My cousins live on the ________________ of town on a large block.

When you are packing for the camp, check that all your ________________, including your ________________, are tagged with your name.

________________ on winning the poetry contest!

Would you mind using your ________________ or turning down the volume?

Use the ________________ to get the meat off the barbecue.

Answer: b

Unit 15

What does vertiginous mean?

a vertical
b whirling
c a virtual reality game show

Say Listen Look Understand Remember Practise

- wondrous ______
- humorous ______
- perilous ______
- miraculous ______
- Indigenous ______
- cantankerous ______
- studious ______
- gregarious ______
- rebellious ______
- voracious ______
- precarious ______
- instantaneous ______
- spontaneous ______
- righteous ______
- ambiguous ______

Tip Sometimes the base word changes when **ous** is added.

1 Look at the base word. Write the related list word, then state the change to the base word.

base word	list word	change to base word
wonder		delete ___
humour		delete ___
miracle		change le to ___
study		change ___ to ___
rebel		double ___

2 Write the two list words that have no change to the base word when **ous** is added.

______ ______

Rule If the base word ends in **ce** or **y**, change **e** or **y** to **i** before adding **ous**.
fury → furious *vice → vicious*

3 Add **ous**.

study	______	grace	______	glory	______
envy	______	mystery	______	luxury	______
malice	______	space	______	fury	______

Rule If the base word ends in **e**, drop the **e** before adding **ous**. *fame → famous*
Exception: some words ending in **ge** *courage → courageous*

4 Add **ous**.

ridicule	______	courage	______	outrage	______
carnivore	______	nerve	______	advantage	______

Spelling Rules! Student Book 6 (ISBN 9780655092728) © Janelle Ho, Helen Pearson

Similes describe something by comparing it to something else using *like* or *as*.
The old building looked as precarious as a house of cards.

5 Write a simile for each word: *suspicious, gregarious, miraculous.*

____

____

____

6 Write the list word that is a synonym. What does the final word mean?

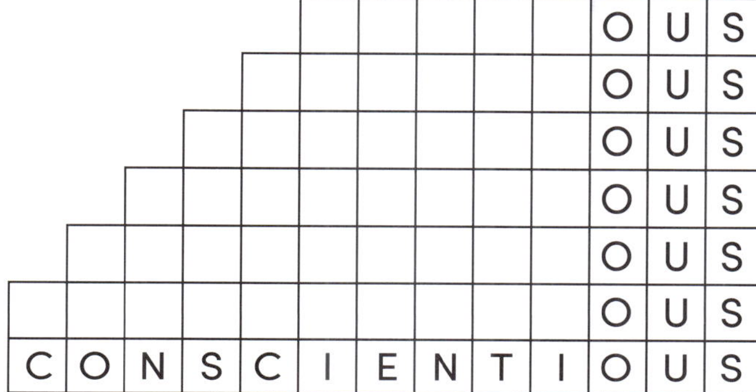

dangerous
greedy
Aboriginal
impulsive
grumpy
immediate

____

7 Use each clue to find a smaller word within a list word. Write the small word and the list word.

clue	answer	list word
something you can ring	________	________
a browning of the skin	________	________
first in a race	________	________
a passenger vehicle	________	________
to sing without words	________	________
large	________	________
move soil with a spade	________	________

8 The words Indigenous and Aboriginal are sometimes used as if they mean the same thing. Find out the difference and explain it in your own words.

____

____

____

Answer: b

Unit 16

What does the word element **neo** mean?

a nil
b new
c a broken neon light

Say **L**isten **L**ook **U**nderstand **R**emember **P**ractise

novel ____________
novelty ____________
novice ____________
innovate ____________
innovation ____________
vocal ____________
vocabulary ____________
advocate ____________
vociferous ____________
invoke ____________
provoke ____________
notice ____________
notify ____________
annotate ____________
reminisce ____________

1 Sort the list words into adjectives, verbs and nouns. Some words may belong to more than one group.

verbs

____________ ____________
____________ ____________
____________ ____________
____________ ____________

nouns

____
____
____
____
____
____
____

adjectives

____
____
____

Most English words have Old English, Latin or Greek origins. Synonyms often have different origins. For example, *new* is from Old English, while *novel* is from Latin. The Latin origins for the list words are:

nova = new *vox* = voice *notare* = note *reminisci* = remember

2 Group the list words.

related to **voice**:

____________ ____________
____________ ____________
____________ ____________

related to **note**: ____________
____________ ____________

related to **remember**:

____

related to **new**:

____________ ____________
____________ ____________
____

Spelling Rules! Student Book 6 (ISBN 9780655092728) © Janelle Ho, Helen Pearson

3 Using the word origin as a clue, write a list word to match each definition.

speaking with a loud, fierce voice ______________

someone new and inexperienced ______________

to produce something new ______________

to call forth ______________

to make notes ______________

to remember the past ______________

to speak on someone's behalf ______________

something new and unusual ______________

4 These words belong to the same word family as list words. Use each word in a sentence to show its meaning. Choose another list word and write a related word and sentence of your own.

renovation: ____

notorious: ____

revoke: ____

reminiscent: ____

______________ ____

Tip **Novel** is a homograph. It has two different meanings.

5 Write a definition for each meaning of *novel*.

novel (noun) = ____

novel (adjective) = ____

6 Use a list word to complete each title. Mcke up a title and author of your own.

A Complete ______________ by B Ginner

______________ No More! by I Forget

______________ in the Home by Han D Man

The ______________ Speaker by IM Noisy

Creating a Great ______________ by Rider Book

______________________________ by ______________________

Answer: b

Unit 17

What is an important rule when you're in a **laboratory**?

a Be careful!
b Have fun!
c Try everything!

Say **L**isten **L**ook **U**nderstand **R**emember **P**ractise

solution	______
toxic	______
method	______
experiment	______
acid	______
alkaline	______
temperature	______
evaporate	______
thermometer	______
theory	______
equipment	______
chemical	______
microscope	______
hypothesis	______
laboratory	______

1 Divide these list words into syllables. Underline the syllable that is stressed in each word.

method	alkaline
evaporate	equipment
microscope	hypothesis
temperature	acid

ic is a less common suffix that changes a noun to an adjective. The base word usually changes when **ic** is added.
tragedy → *tragic*

2 Add **ic** to make the adjective. The base word may change. Use a dictionary if you need help.

noun	adjective
base	
acid	
toxin	
science	
horror	

Tip In a compound word, both parts can be used independently. Some words are not compound words, but consist of two separate word elements. **Scope** and **meter** can act as words and as word elements. As word elements, **scope** refers to a viewing instrument and **meter** to a measuring instrument.

3 Use a dictionary to find the meaning of the word element and the whole word.

micro = ______ microscope = ______
thermo = ______ thermometer = ______

Write other words you know that use these word elements.

scope: ______
meter: ______

4 Write the correct form of a list word to complete each sentence.

What usually makes people sick are ______________ creatures called viruses and bacteria.

When you bake a cake, it is very important to follow the ______________ given in the recipe.

Some ______________ are poisonous. Bottles containing dangerous materials are usually labelled ______________.

My teacher believes that any place can be a ______________. She encourages us to carry out ______________ to test things out. I am going to test my ______________ that the warmer the room, the quicker a slice of apple goes brown.

5 Use list words to complete the puzzle.

Across

6. a room in which experiments are performed
8. a way of explaining what is observed
9. a way of testing a theory

Down

1. a measure of how hot or cold something is
2. a solution is either neutral, acidic or ________
3. good experiments follow the scientific ________
4. to convert a liquid into a gas
5. what is tested during an experiment
7. vinegar is a common ________
10. poisonous

6 Write whether these word pairs are similar or different in meaning.

acidic/alkaline ______________

evaporation/condensation ______________

hypothesis/theory ______________

equipment/apparatus ______________

theoretical/practical ______________

problem/difficulty ______________

Answer: a

Unit 18 Revision

The word quadrumanous is used to describe:

a lions that have four manes
b animals that use four feet as hands
c animals that have four teeth for eating

1 Complete the tables.

noun	adjective
miracle	
advantage	
humour	
mystery	
peculiarity	
essence	
practice	

verb	noun
edit	
equip	
solve	

verb	adjective
despise	
rebel	
innovate	

2 Write words that follow each rule.

Remove silent **e** from the base word before adding a suffix.

____

Change the final **y** to **i** before adding a suffix.

____

Keep the **e** so **g** stays soft when adding a suffix.

____

3 Write the correct form of the verb to complete each sentence.

Dad was ____________ (notify) that he has jury duty next month.

Uncle Carlos ____________ (rebel) against all the rules when he was young but now he's a police inspector!

I love the cakes at Pierre's Patisserie because they are always ____________ (experiment) with new flavours.

Did you know that if you drink too much water, you can get water ____________ (poison)?

Because the water ____________ (evaporate) as soon as it hit the pan, I knew the pan was hot.

At Christmas, our two sets of grandparents love ____________ (reminisce) about their childhoods.

4 Use a word you have learnt to complete each sentence.

Galileo Galilei was the first person to use the ________________ to look at objects in the sky.

Anton van Leeuwenhoek was the first person to observe bacteria under a ________________.

You must take precautions when handling ________________ chemicals.

The best way to increase your ________________ is to read a lot.

A stomach bug gave Ramon a bad case of ________________.

Cherie is always happy to give her ________________ on any issue.

Tip When two or more words start with the same sound, it is called **alliteration**.

5 Write a second word so that each pair is an example of alliteration.

hideous ________________	________________ occasion
peculiar ________________	________________ vehicle
spontaneous ________________	________________ laboratory

6 Write a word to name each category.

	car, truck, tractor, van
	granola, oats, porridge, muesli
	chlorine, ammonia, sodium chloride, fluoride

7 Proofread this text. The text has six words that are incorrect. Circle the mistakes. Then write the correct spelling of the words in the boxes.

The scientist was carrying out an experiment in her laborratory. She had a hypothises to test. Her method was to combine an acid and an alkali in different proportions and measure the temperature at which the solution boiled with a digital thermommeter. She wandered if the results would confirm her theorey that newtral solutions had the highest boiling point.

Answer: b

Unit 19

Flocculation is what happens when:

a music makes you sway from side to side
b flocks of sheep gather
c things are formed in a woolly mass

Say Listen Look Understand Remember Practise

definition ____________
repetition ____________
condemnation ____________
alteration ____________
interpretation ____________
continuation ____________
declaration ____________
cancellation ____________
inflammation ____________
explanation ____________
exclamation ____________
variation ____________
identification ____________
notification ____________
clarification ____________

1 Complete the table.

verb	noun
satisfy	
define	
	cancellation
	declaration
	exclamation
alter	
	repetition
	continuation

Rule

To add **ion** to a base word ending in **y**, change the **y** to **i** and add **cation**.
multiply → multiplication
Some exceptions: *vary → variation*
satisfy → satisfaction

2 Complete the tables.

base word	add ion	base word	add ion
apply		notify	
multiply		magnify	
identify		clarify	

3 Write a list word.

This list word has a silent letter in its base word. ____________

This list word doubles the final consonant in its base word. ____________

4 Write the noun form for each verb. Say each pair aloud.

inflame ____________ classify ____________ define ____________

What happens to the stress on the final syllable? ____________

____

5 *Convert* and *converse* both form a noun ending in **ion**. Write the nouns, then use each one in a sentence. Use a dictionary if you need help.

convert ____________________

____

converse ____________________

____

6 Use the clues to complete the puzzle.

Puzzle	Clue
_ _ _ I O N	all talk and no ________
_ _ _ _ I O N	learning with a tutor
_ _ _ _ _ I O N	The judge's ________ is final.
_ _ _ _ _ _ I O N	antonym of acceptance
_ _ _ _ _ _ _ I O N	what someone makes when they accuse you of something
_ _ _ _ _ _ _ _ I O N	What is your ________ for being late?
_ _ _ _ _ _ _ _ _ I O N	document that informs you of something

Tip

An **abbreviation** is either a short form of a word, or the first letter of each word in a phrase.
government → govt   *United States of America → USA*
An **acronym** is a special kind of abbreviation. In an acronym, the abbreviation is pronounced as a whole word.
AIDS   *PIN*

7 Write the abbreviated name of each organisation. Circle the abbreviations that are acronyms.

United Nations Educational, Scientific and Cultural Organization ____________________
International Union for Conservation of Nature ____________________
Royal Society for the Prevention of Cruelty to Animals ____________________
North Atlantic Treaty Organization ____________________
National Aeronautic and Space Administration ____________________
International Crime Police Organization ____________________

8 What is odd about these phrases that contain an abbreviation?

ATM machine   HIV virus   PIN number

____

____

____

Answer: c

Unit 20

An aviary is where:

a aircraft are designed
b honey is harvested
c birds are kept

Say Listen Look Understand Remember Practise

military	________
anniversary	________
solitary	________
documentary	________
contrary	________
crockery	________
confectionery	________
surgery	________
nursery	________
treachery	________
forgery	________
sensory	________
contradictory	________
category	________
exploratory	________

1 Complete the table.

list word	adjective, noun or both?
crockery	
secondary	
nursery	
solitary	
treachery	
forgery	
anniversary	
military	

Tip

Some words can be pronounced in two ways and in one way, a syllable is not pronounced.
For example, *dormitory* can be pronounced as *daw-muh-tuh-ry* or *daw-muh-try*.
A syllable that is not pronounced is **elided**.

2 These words can be pronounced in two ways. Circle the syllable that can be elided.

category secretary jewellery desperate

3 Write a word ending in **ary** or **ery** to complete each advertising slogan.

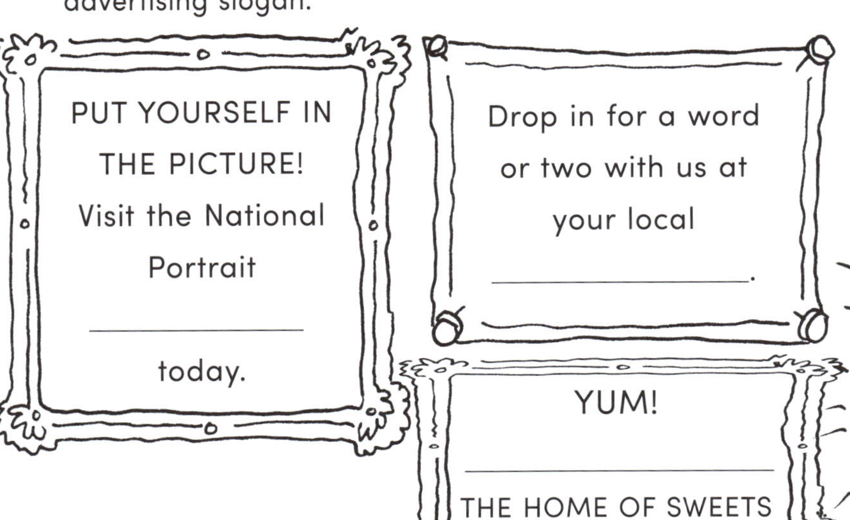

There's no present like the time!
Watch out for specials at Clocks 'n' Gems ________.

Spelling Rules! Student Book 6 (ISBN 9780655092728) © Janelle Ho, Helen Pearson

4 Write a list word that names the category.

__________ army, navy, air force

__________ cakes, sweets, chocolates

__________ plates, bowls, cups, saucers

__________ flowers, shrubs, saplings

Write a list word that is part of the category.

birthday, graduation, wedding, __________

fake, fraud, counterfeit, __________

classification, group, class, __________

pre-school, daycare centre, school, __________

Which word is used twice? __________

This word has two different meanings. Such a word is known as a __________.

5 Use *stationary* or *stationery* to complete each sentence.

The doors will not open until the bus is __________.

Where's the cheapest place to buy the __________ I need for school?

Some satellites are geo__________ in their orbit.

6 Add **ary**, **ery** or **ory**.

diction___	bound___	lavat___	secret___	laborat___	the___
hist___	imag___	lott___	burgl___	necess___	volunt___

7 Proofread this text. The text has five words that are incorrect. Circle the mistakes. Then write the correct spelling of the words in the boxes.

I love books, and one day I'd like to work in a libary. I think I'd enjoy putting each new book into its correct categry. I'm not sure what the salery would be. To become a librarian you have to finish secondory school first, and then go to university. I think I'll try doing work experience to make sure that the benefits aren't just imaginery!

Answer: c

Unit 21

The World Health Organization (WHO) defines an **ad**olescent as being

a 6–10 years old
b 10–19 years old
c 18–24 years old

Say **L**isten **L**ook **U**nderstand **R**emember **P**ractise

anew	________
akin	________
avert	________
abduct	________
abhor	________
abnormal	________
abolish	________
abrupt	________
abuse	________
adhere	________
adolescent	________
adversary	________
accelerate	________
accumulate	________
acquit	________

Tip The prefix **ab-** means *away from* or *opposite to.*

Tip The prefix **a-** means two things:
1. in, on, towards *run aground*
2. in a state of *asleep*

1 Write a sentence using the list word.

anew: one more time

____

____

akin: related by blood; similar to

____

____

2 Write words beginning with **a-** to complete the paragraph.

Rhea set the toy boat ____________ in the pool. She was taken ____________ when Jon said she wasn't allowed to play with it. She called her father. Dad took Jon ____________ and told him to return Rhea the boat.

3 Use the etymology to write a list word. Then write its meaning.

ab + *uti* (use) = ____

____

ab + *norma* (rule) = ____

____

ab + *rumpere* (break) = ____

____

ab + *horrere* (tremble at) = ____

____

ab + *ducere* (lead) = ____

____

The prefix **ad-** means *towards*. Its spelling changes to **ac-** before the letters **c** or **q**.

4 Write **ad** or **ac**.

___cent	___dress	___vertise	___count	___here	___mit
___quire	___celerate	___monish	___claim	___quit	___olescent

5 Write a list word that is a synonym.

prevent ________	attach ________	kidnap ________
afresh ________	strange ________	quicken ________

6 Write a list word that is an antonym.

spend ________	love ________	different ________
convict ________	friend ________	unhurried ________

7 The words *avert*, *averse* and *adverse* are easy to confuse.
Use the example sentences to write a sentence of your own.

The teacher averted disaster by herding the children outdoors.

____

____

I'm not averse to going on the tree walk as long as you promise not to shake the bridge.

____

____

Jenna's not feeling well. Let's just say she had an adverse reaction to too many lamingtons!

____

____

8 Write a story about a character's conflict with an adversary. It can be a personal true story or an imaginary one.

____

____

____

____

____

____

____

____

Answer: b

Unit 22

A heckel**phone** is:

a a loud heckler
b a noisy telephone
c a musical instrument

Say Listen Look Understand Remember Practise

symphony ______
phonetic ______
microphone ______
cacophony ______
synonym ______
antonym ______
pseudonym ______
anonymous ______
empathy ______
telepathy ______
majesty ______
majority ______
magnify ______
magnificent ______
magnanimous ______

1 Write a list word that rhymes.

athletic ______
priority ______
synonymous ______

2 Write a list word that contains the smaller word.

net ______	cop ______
crop ______	ice ______
jest ______	one ______
pat ______ ______	cent ______
	or ______

3 Write whether these word pairs are synonyms or antonyms. Then write your own examples of synonyms and antonyms.

	synonyms or antonyms?	your examples
majority/most	______	______
magnanimous/petty	______	______

4 Write a word that has the same underlined word element.

<u>micro</u>phone ______ <u>ma</u>jesty ______ <u>tele</u>pathy ______

5 Circle the meaning of each word element.

micro	loud	small	measure
magni	great	royal	magic
tele	sound	sender	far away

Spelling Rules! Student Book 6 (ISBN 9780655092728) © Janelle Ho, Helen Pearson

6 The meaning of each word element is given. **L** or **G** shows whether the word is from Latin or Greek. Write the list word that combines these word elements.

tele G: *far away*	+	patheia G: *feeling*	=	____________
kako G: *bad*	+	phone G: *sound*	=	____________
syn G: *together*	+	onyma G: *name*	=	____________
anti G: *opposite*	+	onyma G: *name*	=	____________
pseudo G: *false*	+	onyma G: *name*	=	____________
em L: *in*	+	patheia G: *feeling*	=	____________
poly G: *many*	+	phonic G: *sound*	=	____________
magnus L: *great*	+	animus L: *soul*	=	____________

7 Circle the malapropism in each sentence and write the correct word.

The magician claimed he used mental telegraphy to communicate with his assistant. ____________

The kidnapper sent a synonymous letter demanding a huge ransom. ____________

The authority of the class voted to play volleyball in the gym. ____________

Sam wears glasses to modify the text on his laptop. ____________

8 Rewrite each sentence using the correct form of a list word to make it shorter.

Dictionaries often use an alphabet in which symbols replace letters to represent pronunciation.

____

Being able to walk in others' shoes helps us understand them better.

____

Being on stage is scary because the silence makes every mistake seem bigger.

____

Answer: c

Unit 23

WHO is the abbreviation for:

a World Health Organization
b World Horticultural Organisation
c Wild Horses in the Outback

Say Listen Look Understand Remember Practise	
medicine	______
bacteria	______
virus	______
pregnant	______
fracture	______
organ	______
influenza	______
abdomen	______
intestine	______
capsule	______
appendix	______
vaccination	______
immunisation	______
pneumonia	______
stethoscope	______

1 Write list words to complete the table.

Category	Examples
	antibiotics, aspirin, ______
medical equipment	syringe, thermometer, ______
	heart, lungs, ______
illnesses	bronchitis, tonsillitis, ______

2 Write list words to answer the questions.

Which word has a silent letter? ______

Which words end in the same vowel sound?

______ ______ ______

Which words have a soft **c** sound?

______ ______

Which words contain double letters?

______ ______ ______

3 Use each clue to find a smaller word within a list word. Write the small word and the list word.

clue	answer	list word
an assessment task	______	______
a shape like a hemisphere	______	______
a type of hat	______	______
a strong but tiny insect	______	______
a tool for writing	______	______
to play a part	______	______
rested on a chair	______	______

Spelling Rules! Student Book 6 (ISBN 9780655092728) © Janelle Ho, Helen Pearson

The word *organ* is a homograph. The word *appendix* is also a homograph. Each word has two very different meanings.

4 Write sentences to show the different meanings of *organ* and *appendix*. Use a dictionary if you need help.

organ 1. ______________________

2. ______________________

appendix 1. ______________________

2. ______________________

5 Say each word aloud. Which word does not belong? Why not?

chronic fracture medical stomach muscle ache bacteria

____

6 Write what each abbreviation stands for. Circle the abbreviations that are acronyms.

flu ______________ CF ______________

AIDS ______________ ADD ______________

MS ______________ SIDS ______________

7 Each sentence contains one or two spelling errors. Circle the mistakes and write each word correctly.

I have a pain in my apendix so I have a docter's appointment. ______________ ______________

Salim fracturd his wrist attempting to catch a cricket ball. ______________

We thought our cat's swelling addomen meant she was overweight, but it turned out she was pregnent. ______________ ______________

Nowadays children can be imunnised against many diseases. ______________

Why is it that even in hot whether a stethescope feels cold on your chest? ______________ ______________

If you have asthma, the wheeze makes it hard to breath. ______________

8 Write about a day in the life of a doctor. Use as many list words as you can.

____

____

____

____

Answer: a

Unit 24 Revision

What is sterilis**ation**?

a staring all the time
b the realisation that you do not like stairs
c the process of making something free of germs

1 Write the plural.

symphony ______
multiple ______
bacterium ______
virus ______
adolescent ______

2 Write the past tense.

vaccinate ______
magnify ______
acquit ______
abhor ______
yearn ______

3 Add a suffix to each verb to complete the tables.

verb	noun
exclaim	
continue	
define	
satisfy	
repeat	

verb	noun
condemn	
imagine	
vary	
document	
categorise	

4 Write the list words from Units 19–23 that have silent letters.

______ ______

5 Name these instruments used by a doctor.

______ ______

6 Write the double letters to complete each word.

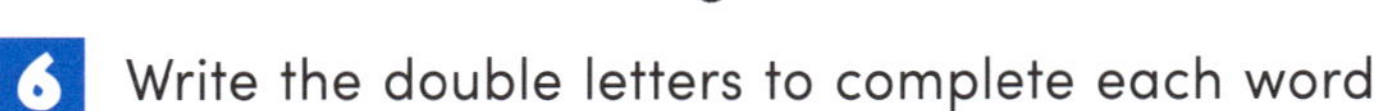
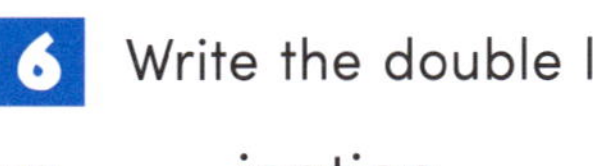

va __ __ ination   a __ __ iversary   i __ __ ovate   a __ __ endix
i __ __ unisation   a __ __ elerate   misce __ __ aneous   cance __ __ ation

7 Fill in the letters that make the **schwa** sound.

__ brupt   org __ n   vir __ s   alt __ rat __ n   categ __ ry
telep __ thy   medic __ ne   abdom __ n   __ new   fract __

8 Add **ary**, **ery** or **ory**.

libr___   groc___   document___   forg___   summ___   explorat___
dormit___   jewell___   second___   gall___   imagin___   laborat___

9 Some letters have gone missing from each sentence. Write each sentence correctly.

At the begning of my project I have t includ a sumry.

____

Kara's favrit game is Monopoly becase she can be an imaginry millonaire.

____

Mr Jaffar is forgtful and somtimes throws his medcines away.

____

I was feeling mananimus so I forgave Rita for eating the majorty of the cofectionry.

____

10 Use the clues to complete the puzzle.

1.				A								
2.		A		A								
3.					A							
4.	A						A					
5.		A										
6.	A					A						
7.									A			
8.											A	

1. a musical instrument or body part
2. money for doing work
3. a place to borrow books
4. strange
5. a series of loud grating noises
6. a charge made against you
7. a movie that gives information
8. speaking many languages

11 Write a word to complete each riddle.

Q: Why did the boy tiptoe past the medicine cabinet?

A: He didn't want to wake the ______________ tablets.

Q: Why is an optometrist like a teacher?

A: They both examine the ______________.

12 Write the correct form of each word to complete the sentences.

I fell down the stairs the other day and ______________ my ankle.
(fracture)

Roald is great at addition, subtraction and division, but not as good at ______________.
(multiply)

The car ______________ ______________ and made me spill my drink.
(accelerate) (abrupt)

Answer: c

Unit 25

A **cygnet** is:

a a baby swan
b a tubular fishing net
c an internet expert

Say Listen Look Understand Remember Practise	
cyclone	____
cynical	____
cyberspace	____
urgency	____
accuracy	____
literacy	____
numeracy	____
privacy	____
pregnancy	____
diplomacy	____
adequacy	____
delicacy	____
obstinacy	____
buoyancy	____
legacy	____

1 Circle the word in which **cy** has a different sound.

cyclone cynical cyberspace

2 Use letters from each word to make a smaller word in which **c** has a hard sound. Use as many letters as you can.

cyclone	numeracy	obstinacy
____	____	____
pregnancy	legacy	privacy
____	____	____

3 Fill in words ending in **cy**.

The Chinese ____ is the yuan.
The motel's sign read 'No ____'.
The flood caused ____ evacuations.
A ____ lasts about nine months.

Rule

Most nouns ending in **cy** have base words ending in **nt** or **te**.

infant → infancy *delicate → delicacy*

4 Write the base word.

accuracy	urgency	obstinacy	buoyancy
____	____	____	____
privacy	adequacy	numeracy	literacy
____	____	____	____

5 What is the base word of **cy**nical? Use a dictionary to find a related word to complete each sentence.

A person who is cynical is called a ____.
A person who is cynical suffers from ____.

Spelling Rules! Student Book 6 (ISBN 9780655092728) © Janelle Ho, Helen Pearson

Cyber is a word element that shows that the word is related to computers.

6 Write a word beginning with **cyber** to match each definition.

_______________ a place where you can eat and use the internet at the same time

_______________ the irrational fear of computers or technology

7 Write list words.

Caviar is considered a _______________ in many countries.

Reading and writing are _______________ skills.

Air increases the _______________ of an inflatable object and helps it float.

People who value their _______________ often grow tall hedges.

_______________ Tracy caused great devastation in Darwin in 1974.

After practising archery for many months, my _______________ improved.

International _______________ resulted in a peace treaty.

The engineer advised that a new bridge should be built with _______________.

Tip The prefix **ob** is Greek in origin and can mean either *towards* or *against*.

8 Each word in the puzzle begins with **ob**. Use a dictionary if you need help.

1.	O	B									
2.	O	B									
3.	O	B									
4.	O	B									
5.	O	B									
6.	O	B									
7.	O	B									
8.	O	B									
9.	O	B									
10.	O	B									

1. significantly overweight
2. to focus irrational attention on
3. to get or acquire
4. to watch closely
5. unclear or hidden
6. to put an obstacle in the way
7. out of date
8. clearly, evidently
9. an offensive or indecent word or remark
10. antonym of subjectivity

Answer: a

Unit 26

Psittacism is:

a an intelligent joke
b the habit of sitting around all the time
c meaningless, repetitive babble

Say Listen Look Understand Remember Practise

territory ______
graffiti ______
suppress ______
pallor ______
assassin ______
apparatus ______
millennium ______
succulent ______
eccentric ______
gimmick ______
dilemma ______
pinnacle ______
abbreviation ______
etiquette ______
intermittent ______

1 Write each word as prefix + base word. What do you notice about the double letters?

unnecessary ______
immigration ______
irregular ______
dissatisfied ______
cooperation ______
surreal ______

2 Complete the table.

verb	add ing
suffocate	
suppress	
interrogate	
suffice	
recommend	
terrorise	

3 Underline the stressed syllable in each word.

territory intermittent graffiti pallor eccentric
etiquette curriculum succulent suppress apparatus

4 Sort the list words according to the number of syllables.

2
______
______
______

3
______
______
______
______
______
______
______

4
______
______
______
______

Which word is left?

______

5 Write a list word that is a synonym.

manners ____________

stunt ____________

peak ____________

6 Write one word for each period of time.

10 years ____________

100 years ____________

1000 years ____________

Tip Nouns ending in **us** or **um** are Latin in origin. The Latin plural forms are still sometimes used. *radius* → *radii* *datum* → *data*
But nowadays most words add **s** or **es** to make the plural.
virus → *viruses* *vacuum* → *vacuums*

7 Write the plural without adding **s**. Use a dictionary to check your answer.

fungus	cactus	curriculum	millennium	crisis
____________	____________	____________	____________	____________

8 Which list word is French? ____________

9 Use the correct form of a list word to complete each sentence.

Many animals are ____________ by nature. Once they have established their ____________, they will fight others to protect it.

Both the peach and the nectarine look so ____________ that I have a ____________ about which to eat.

Meg found it hard to sleep because the streetlight outside her window would flash ____________.

Our school painted a mural on the fence to prevent ____________.

US President John F Kennedy was ____________ in Dallas in 1963.

The scientific ____________ in the laboratory included beakers, test tubes and Bunsen burners.

Tip **Collective nouns** can be conventional or creative.
a school of fish *a wail of weeping willows*

10 Write creative collective nouns for *confetti* and *graffiti*. Then choose two words of your own and write collective nouns for them.

word	collective noun
confetti	
graffiti	

Unit 27

A **suf**fragette is a

a female supporter of women's voting rights
b person who suffers greatly
c female farmer who grows courgettes

Say **L**isten **L**ook **U**nderstand **R**emember **P**ractise

subconscious	______
sublime	______
submerge	______
subordinate	______
subside	______
substandard	______
subterranean	______
subtle	______
succinct	______
succumb	______
suffocate	______
suppose	______
supplement	______
surreptitious	______
suspend	______

1 Write a list word that answers the questions.

Which two words have a silent letter?

______ ______

In which word is **cc** pronounced as in accelerate?

______

In which word is **cc** pronounced as in account?

______

Which two words have the same last syllable?

______ ______

Tip The prefix **sub-** means *under* or *less than*. The letter **b** may change to match the beginning consonant of the base word.

2 Write the correct spelling of the prefix **sub-**.

____total	____merge	____press
____cumb	____plement	____conscious
____pose	____port	____divide
____fix	____ficient	____scribe
____stance	____ceed	____ply

3 Colour A if the word is an adjective, V if the word is a verb or N if the word is a noun.

subconscious A V N	sublime A V N	submerge A V N
subordinate A V N	subside A V N	substandard A V N
subterranean A V N	subtle A V N	succinct A V N
succumb A V N	suffocate A V N	suppose A V N
supplement A V N	surreptitious A V N	suspend A V N

Spelling Rules! Student Book 6 (ISBN 9780655092728) © Janelle Ho, Helen Pearson

4 Write list words to complete the puzzle. Write your own clue for each word.

Down

1. ____________________
2. ____________________
4. ____________________
5. ____________________
7. ____________________
8. ____________________
9. ____________________
11. ____________________
12. ____________________

Across

2. ____________________
3. ____________________
6. ____________________
10. ____________________
13. ____________________
14. ____________________

5 Write list words to match the clues.

This word has a pet in it. ____________________

This word is below the earth. ____________________

This word goes underwater. ____________________

This word has a writing instrument in it. ____________________

This word is short and sweet. ____________________

This word is glorious. ____________________

This word is just not good enough. ____________________

Answer: a

Unit 28

A **dis**incentive is:

a a process that removes smells
b a machine that takes away your coins
c something that discourages you from doing something

Say Listen Look Understand Remember Practise

incomprehension ____________
unmanageable ____________
discontinued ____________
ignorance ____________
invisibility ____________
irrational ____________
immobile ____________
immovable ____________
noticeably ____________
symmetrical ____________
unintentionally ____________
uncritically ____________
reversible ____________
illegibly ____________
predestined ____________

1 Add a prefix to make the antonym.

legible	mobile	visible
________	________	________
interested	necessary	rational
________	________	________
continue	critical	reversible
________	________	________

2 Add a suffix to make a noun.

ignore	press
________	________
exclude	visible
________	________
private	selfish
________	________
manage	criticise
________	________

3 Complete the table. The first word in each row is the base word. Add affixes to increase the number of syllables. The first one has been done for you.

Tip The general term for prefixes and suffixes is **affixes**.

1 syllable	2 syllables	3 syllables	4 syllables	5 syllables
		educate	educated	educational
	reverse			
	explore			
	intend			
note				
change				
please				

Spelling Rules! Student Book 6 (ISBN 9780655092728) © Janelle Ho, Helen Pearson

4 These sentences are too negative. Rewrite each sentence so it makes sense.

The note was not too illegible so Mum didn't know what I wanted.

____

Everyone looked puzzled as the conclusion to Rex's speech was not quite illogical.

____

The decision is irreversible if the manager disagrees with it.

____

The space in the hall was hard to rearrange as the chairs were not immovable.

____

The sale of the toy wasn't discontinued after complaints that it was not unsafe.

____

5 Write the correct form of the word to complete each sentence.

Reading ______________ is an important aspect of literacy.
comprehend

In chapter 1, the author clearly indicates that the baby is ______________ to be the hero.
destiny

A new family has moved in next door. There are two children and an ______________ puppy.
affection

To encourage us in our fundraising this year, our teacher showed us a ______________ about the cause we are supporting.
document

I ______________ trod on our cat's tail this morning.
unintentional

Radio telescopes are an important part of the ______________ of space nowadays.
explore

6 Proofread this text. The text has six words that are incorrect. Circle the mistakes. Then write the correct spelling of the words in the boxes.

I'm writing a detective story. My character, Shirl Lock, is a mischevious girl who loves solving mysteries. In the begining, her collection of semi-preceous gems goes missing. Her investergation leads her to view her best friend with suspision. In the end, however, her brother is the culprit. To apologise for his misbehaviour, he gives Shirl a beautiful piece of amber to add to her collection. In this story's sequal, the amber itself disappears.

Answer: c

Unit 29

What is a questionnaire?

a a person who asks pesky questions
b someone who doesn't know how much money they have
c a list of questions

Say **L**isten **L**ook **U**nderstand **R**emember **P**ractise

currency ______
exchange ______
pound ______
euro ______
rupiah ______
baht ______
allowance ______
financial ______
budget ______
discount ______
subsidy ______
purchase ______
expenditure ______
millionaire ______
treasury ______

1 Write each word as a base word and suffix.

millionaire = ______ + ______
allowance = ______ + ______
financial = ______ + ______
treasury = ______ + ______
accountant = ______ + ______

2 Write the plural.

allowance ______
currency ______
exchange ______
subsidy ______
euro ______

3 Some currencies have a special symbol. Write the currency.

¥ ______ ฿ ______
€ ______ £ ______

4 Write a rhyming word.

pound	euro	baht	millionaire
______	______	______	______

5 Use each clue to find a smaller word within a list word. Write the small word and the list word.

clue	small word	list word
helps fish steer	______	______
a flower not yet in bloom	______	______
to run after someone	______	______
king of the jungle	______	______
opposite of high	______	______
finish	______	______
a flat circular object	______	______

6 Write the correct form of the word to complete the sentence.

Toby was ____________ independent when he was eighteen.
financial

The T-shirt her aunt ____________ was too big, so she took it back to the shop to be
purchase
____________.
exchange

Mrs Vazquez says ____________ is important so we know how much money we can spend
budget
without getting into debt.

The boxes of chocolates were ____________ so Mr Muthu bought ten!
discount

Some generous parents are ____________ our excursion to Uluru.
subsidy

7 These people work with money. Write the occupation to match the definition.

accountant cashier teller money changer

You pay this person at the checkout counter. ____________

You give or receive money from this person in a bank. ____________

This person exchanges one currency for another. ____________

This person keeps track of money in a business. ____________

8 Look at Alex's weekly account and write a report of his budget and expenditure.

Allowance	$20
Savings	$45.60
Magazine	$4.50
Grandma's gift	$7.50
Computer game	$6.95
Pool entry	$3.00
Ice cream	$2.70
	$24.65

____
____
____
____
____
____

Answer: c

Unit 30 Revision

To rappel is to:

a rap without a sense of rhythm
b descend a steep slope using a rope
c turn magnets away from each other

1 These words need single or double consonants added. Write the words correctly using the consonants in brackets.

su__u__ent (c, l) | va__i__ation (c, n) | a__o__odation (c, m)

a__a__in (s, s) | gra__i__i (f, t) | de__e__io__ate (t, r, r)

cu__i__u__um (r, c, l) | a__e__ible (c, s) | o__a__iona__y (c, s, l)

2 Write the plural.

territory	committee	millennium	dilemma	currency
________	________	________	________	________

3 Most of the vowels have been left out of these sentences. Write each sentence correctly.

My sstr s xtrmly obstnt so w cn rrly prsd hr t chng hr mnd.

____

____

Prsnlly, I thnk m ncl is a lttl ccntrc bcs h njys rdng th dctnry.

____

____

I m rsrchng th dffrnc n tmpratur f bjcts dpndng on hw lng thy hve bn sbmrgd.

____

____

4 Write the correct form of the words to complete each sentence. You will need to add either one or two affixes.

Diana tried ________ (success) to thread a needle and felt ________ (frustrate) when she pricked her finger yet again.

Faizal is an ________ (accomplish) ________ (violin). So far, his greatest ________ (achieve) has been ________ (perform) at the Town Hall.

As a result of food ________ (poison), her ________ (immune) was low and she ________ (succumb) to a bout of influenza.

Jill ________ (try) to claim ________ (ignore) but the judge was ________ (sympathy) and said her actions were ________ (excuse).

Spelling Rules! Student Book 6 (ISBN 9780655092728) © Janelle Ho, Helen Pearson

5 Write a word to match each definition. Each word has the letters **cy**, but not as a suffix.

hurricane ______________

two-wheeled transportation ______________

a conical, evergreen tree ______________

use again ______________

book of knowledge ______________

a poison ______________

6 Write a synonym and an antonym.

	synonym	**antonym**
buy	______________	______________
new	______________	______________
rational	______________	______________
sufficient	______________	______________

7 Write the correct form of the word to complete each sentence.

I closed my door to get some ______________. (private)

Please check your work for ______________. (accurate)

Snails are considered a ______________ in France. (delicate)

Objects have greater ______________ in salt water than in fresh water. (buoyant)

8 Add **c**, **cc**, **x** or **xc**.

o___upation	su___essful	e___ercise	de___ide
e___entric	re___eive	e___tra	a___entuate
e___cite	a___complish	e___ept	e___act

9 Write as many words as you can by adding affixes to the base word. Choose one member of the word family to use in your own sentence.

able ____

____

believe ____

____

excite ____

____

Answer: b

Unit 31

A fa**sci**cle is:

a an interesting fact
b a broken icicle
c a small bundle

Say **L**isten **L**ook **U**nderstand **R**emember **P**ractise

a**sce**nd ____________________
de**sce**nd ____________________
tran**sce**nd ____________________
ob**sce**ne ____________________
adole**sce**nt ____________________
fluore**sce**nt ____________________
iride**sce**nt ____________________
efferve**sce**nt ____________________
mi**sce**llaneous ____________________
su**sce**ptible ____________________
convale**sce** ____________________
scintillate ____________________
con**sci**ence ____________________
con**sci**entious ____________________
resu**sci**tate ____________________

1 Each word has a soft **c** sound. Use some of the letters in each word to make a word with a hard **c** sound.

obscene	miscellaneous
____________	____________
susceptible	resuscitate
____________	____________

2 Write the list word that contains the smaller word.

dole	ran
____________	____________
ride	lane
____________	____________
it	science
____________	____________
scene	ale
____________	____________

Tip *Ascend*, *descend* and *transcend* all have the same Latin origin, *scandere*, meaning *to climb*. The prefix **a** or **ad** means *towards*, **de** means *away from* and **trans** means *beyond*.

3 Write what each word means. Use a dictionary to check your answer.

descend = ____________________

ascend = ____________________

transcend = ____________________

4 Use a word containing **sce** or **sci** and alliteration to invent a product name.

*Erin's efferve**sce**nt energy drink*

____

____

Spelling Rules! Student Book 6 (ISBN 9780655092728) © Janelle Ho, Helen Pearson

5 These sets of words are sometimes confused. Write the correct word to complete each sentence.

ascent accent assent

The principal gave his ____________ to our plan to hold a twilight barbecue.
Don told the joke with a French ____________ to make us laugh.
The ____________ of Mount Everest must be made in stages.

descent decent dissent

She's got a ____________ singing voice but she's no opera singer!
Be careful, as the ____________ is steep and muddy.
There was no ____________ when Magda and Ewan were elected school captains.

6 Add the suffix to make the noun.

base word	add ion
fascinate	
resuscitate	

base word	add ity
susceptible	
obscene	

base word	add ence
convalesce	
effervesce	
transcend	
fluoresce	

7 Write the correct form of a list word to complete each sentence.

Grandma is ______________ well after her operation, although she is still ______________ to infection.

The dance troupe put on a ______________ performance at the concert. They wore ______________ costumes that appeared to glow in the spotlights.

Dad contributed many ______________ objects to our school's garage sale – but he bought even more junk home again!

8 Write the list words that have meanings related to light. Use a dictionary if you need help.

____

Choose one of these words and use it in a sentence.

____

Answer: c

Unit 32

Syzygy is:

a a country near Kazakhstan
b the conjunction or opposition of two heavenly bodies
c the noise sausages make when you throw them on a barbecue

Say **L**isten **L**ook **U**nderstand **R**emember **P**ractise

onomatopoeia ________________
asphalt ________________
amateur ________________
havoc ________________
jargon ________________
anemone ________________
flummox ________________
sleuth ________________
nuisance ________________
naive ________________
pizzazz ________________
eclipse ________________
impromptu ________________
labyrinth ________________
conundrum ________________

1 Sort the list words according to the number of syllables. Underline the stressed syllable in each word.

1 ________________

2 ________________
____
____
____
____
____
____
____

3 ________________
____
____
____

4 ________________

5 ________________

2 Break the word into its base word and suffix.

skiing = ____________ + ____________
queued = ____________ + ____________
naively = ____________ + ____________

3 Write list words.

The new puppy caused ________________ when it got into the grocery bags.

They discovered the pungent smell was caused by new ________________ being put down on the road.

An ________________ of the sun is an amazing natural event.

The poet uses ________________ to express the storm's ferocity.

AMAZING

Tip

Mnemonics are tricks to help you remember something more easily.
Eclipse – it ***clips*** *from* ***e*** *to* ***e****.* *With as****th****ma, each brea****th*** *is hard.*

4 Choose three list words you find difficult, then make up a mnemonic for each.

Spelling Rules! Student Book 6 (ISBN 9780655092728) © Janelle Ho, Helen Pearson

5 Write a list word so that the first and last part of each sentence rhymes.

The intrepid ______________ found the thief in a booth.
The saxophonist played jazz with a lot of ______________.
The locusts caused ______________ as they ate through the paddock.
We planned a simple barbecue; the party was quite ______________.

6 Use *nuisance* as an adjective and a noun.

adjective ____

noun ____

7 Circle the malapropism in each sentence. Write the correct word in the box.

The anomalies in the rock pool waved their tentacles.

Keep quiet and don't be such a nuance!

This competition is only open to armchairs.

The compendium was that the suspect couldn't be in two places at one time.

8 Find one word or phrase in each sentence for which a list word is a synonym. Circle the word or phrase you have chosen and write the synonym in the box.

The basement was a maze of storerooms and passageways.

Dad gave an off-the-cuff speech at his birthday dinner.

The article was full of vocabulary that only experts could understand.

Tip

Similes describe something by comparing it to something else using *like* or *as*.
Her hair was like silk.
Metaphors describe something by saying it *is* something else.
Her hair was black silk.

9 Write a simile and a metaphor to describe an eclipse.

simile ____

metaphor ____

Answer: b

Unit 33

An **angklong** is:

a a very long rowboat
b an Indonesian musical instrument
c an angle on the long side of a rectangle

Say **L**isten **L**ook **U**nderstand **R**emember **P**ractise

trek	______
snorkel	______
mammoth	______
deluxe	______
carnival	______
rampage	______
maestro	______
berserk	______
gruesome	______
cologne	______
abseil	______
souvenir	______
gourmet	______
silhouette	______
entrepreneur	______

1 Fill in the silent letters.

gourme_ sil_ouette colo_ne

Tip Some words can be both nouns and verbs.
I ***spy*** *a fly. I didn't know he was a* ***spy****.*

2 Write a sentence for each meaning of these words.

trek (noun): ______

trek (verb): ______

snorkel (noun): ______

snorkel (verb): ______

3 Use a dictionary to find out where each list word comes from.

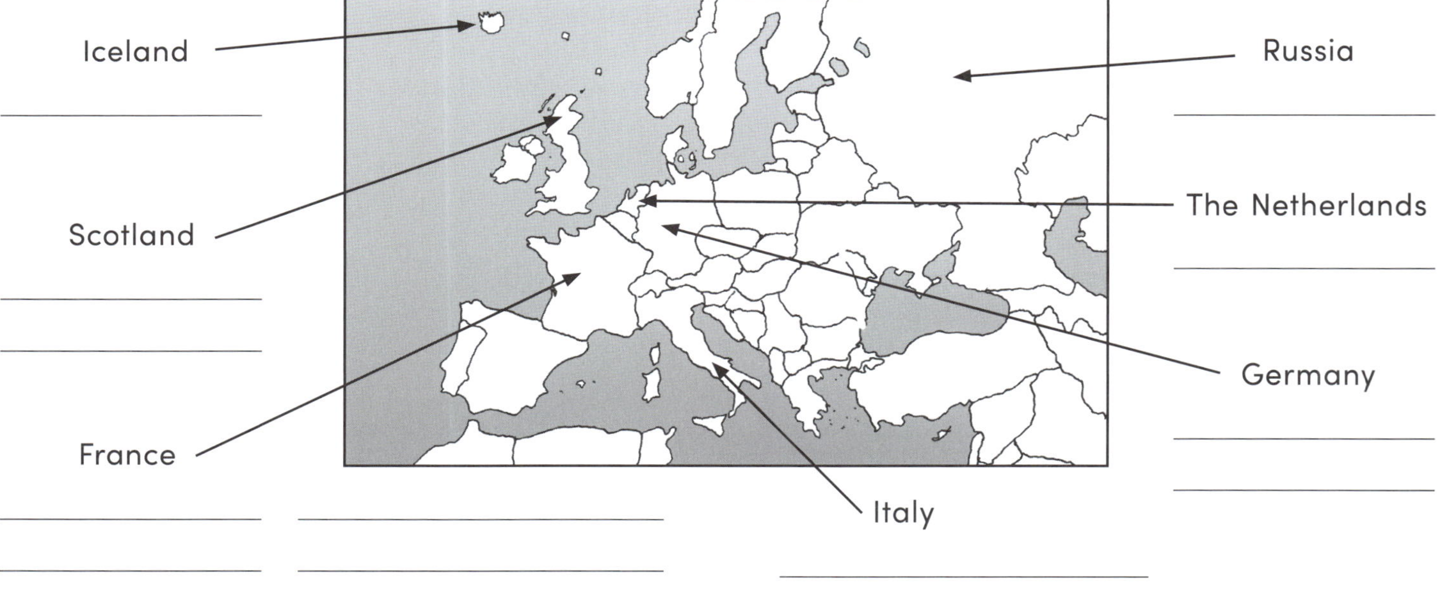

4 Use list words to complete the puzzle.

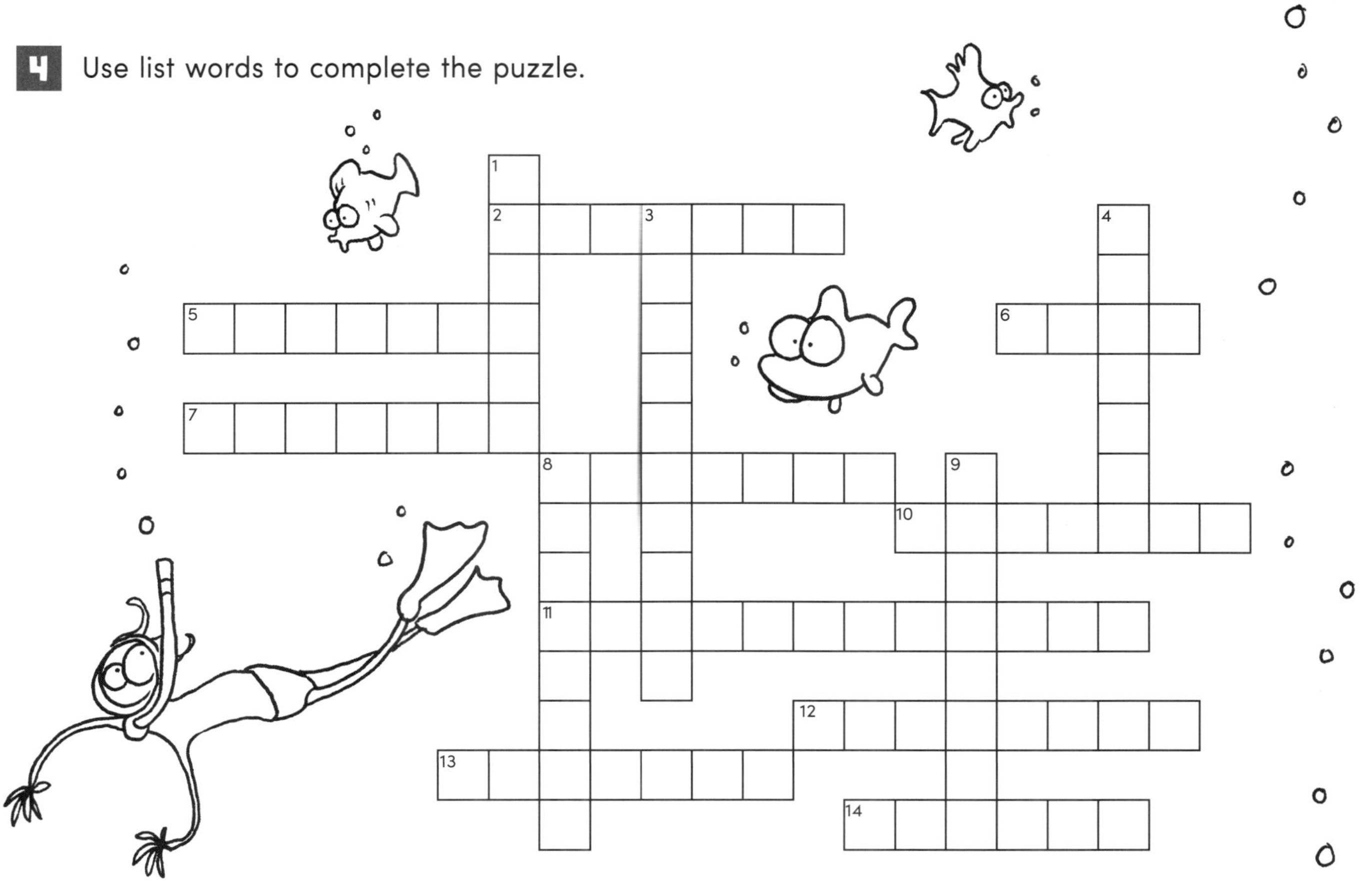

Across

2. wild and frenzied
5. perfume
6. long and difficult journey
7. tube for breathing underwater
8. of excellent taste
10. gigantic
11. business person
12. a holiday keepsake
13. destructive behaviour
14. of superior quality

Down

1. to descend using a rope
3. an outline
4. a distinguished musician
8. horrific
9. a travelling fair or sports meet

5 Write list words you might use when talking about these topics.

war ____________________

sports ____________________

people ____________________

your senses ____________________

Answer: b

Unit 34

An **astro**labe was a medieval instrument used to measure:

a the altitude of the stars and planets
b how much water stars hold
c how many labradors there are in space

Say **L**isten **L**ook **U**nderstand **R**emember **P**ractise

asteroid	____________
astronaut	____________
astronomy	____________
comet	____________
galaxy	____________
meteor	____________
orbit	____________
dimension	____________
futuristic	____________
chronology	____________
medieval	____________
terrestrial	____________
archaeologist	____________
palaeontology	____________
Renaissance	____________

1 Sort the list words according to whether they are related to time or space. Some words may fit both categories.

time: ____________________

____

____

____

____

space: ____________________

____

____

____

____

Write the word that is French in origin and means 'rebirth'.

____

The prefix **astro** comes from the Greek word for *star*.

2 Use the definitions to complete the puzzle.

1.	A	S	T	E	R					
2.	A	S	T	E	R					
3.	A	S	T	R	O					
4.	A	S	T	R	O					
5.	A	S	T	R	O					

1. a structure that revolves around the sun
2. name of the symbol *
3. a space traveller
4. the study of the universe
5. a person who studies the universe

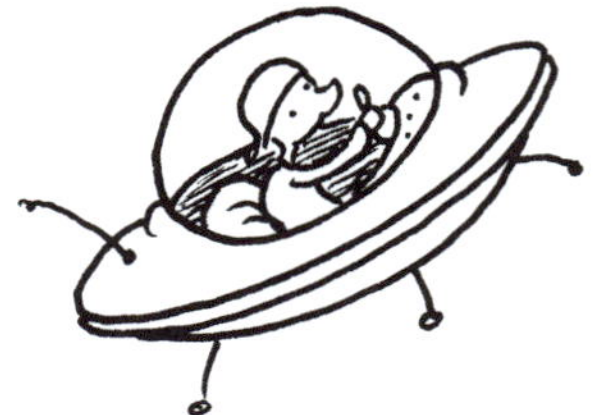

3 Use each clue to find a smaller word within a list word. Write the small word and the list word.

clue	small word	list word
a sphere	____________	____________
opposite of go	____________	____________
male adults	____________	____________
to have a break	____________	____________

An **idiom** is a group of words always used in a fixed expression.

4 Write the meaning of each idiom.

out of this world ______________________________

to work like clockwork ______________________________

par for the course ______________________________

a dog's breakfast ______________________________

in the nick of time ______________________________

know it like the back of your hand ______________________________

5 Write the correct form of a list word to complete each sentence.

Two of the first ____________ to land on the moon were Neil Armstrong and John Glenn.

Takei has had a ____________ rise in the company. He's worked there for only a year and is already a manager.

A ____________ is someone who studies fossils in order to discover more about extinct plants and animals. Part of the job is working out the ____________ order of events so as to trace the evolution of these plants and animals.

A shape like a circle or square is two-____________ because it only has length and breadth. A sphere and a cylinder have three ____________ because they also have depth and can contain things.

Aliens can also be called ____________ creatures. Most movies portray such creatures as frightening.

Answer: a

Unit 35 Revision

One of the longest words in the English language is **floccinaucinihilipilification**. It means:

a having hallucinations about sheep
b climbing hills repeatedly
c the act of estimating something as worthless

1 Write the word for each picture.

________ ________ ________ ________

________ ________ ________ ________

2 Complete the table by building word families.

verb	past tense	noun	adjective	adverb
wonder				
	predicted			
		explosion		
			suspicious	
				decisively

3 Some of the vowels have been left out of these words. Add the missing vowels.

___wkw___rd
___rch___logist
fl___rescent
s___ven___r
t___tion
___rie
baz___r
f___na

4 Some of the consonants have been left out of these words. Add the missing consonants.

ex___e___
enviro___ent
___eumonia
e___erve___ence
fra___ure
bu___et
co___oa
a___lete

5 Write a word to match each definition.

a long piece of music played by a large orchestra ________
someone new and inexperienced ________
able to speak many languages ________
a false name ________
a many-sided shape ________
an act of betrayal ________
pretend someone else's words are your own ________

Para onde vai a quinta-feira?

Was machst du am Abend?

Gdzie się podział Czwartek?

6 Each word has been written as it sounds. Rewrite it correctly.

converless	daybew	show fur	may tree ark
__________	__________	__________	__________
rithum	canserlation	missalayneeus	backteeriah
__________	__________	__________	__________

7 Add **g** or **j**.

ad__acent	avera__e	passen__er	__ustice	ur__ent
re__oice	fra__ile	challen__e	pre__udice	__ud__ement

8 Add the letters that make the **er** sound.

p___manent	v___tual	c___cular	categ___y	dist___b
j___ney	p___l	re___se	c___tesy	b___s___k

9 Add **al**, **el** or **le**.

practic__	seri__	chort__	sequenti__	vehic__
gradu__	parall__	optic__	wrest__	skelet__

10 Circle any words in each sentence that do not make sense. Rewrite each sentence so it makes sense.

The train terminals at the next stop.

____

When I had affluence, the doctor listened to my chest with a periscope.

____

'You'd better have a good exclamation for being late,' said Boris.

____

At dinner, Doug ate an access of dessert. No wonder his digression was affected!

____

We sat on the terrain last night to watch the meter shower.

____

The confetti on the window made it hard to look at the sensory.

____

Answer: c

List words in unit order

Unit 1
genre
geometry
genealogy
gyrate
indulge
grudge
judgement
jubilant
jest
juvenile
junction
hijack
prejudice
adjacent
adjoining

Unit 2
corruption
exhibition
exception
restriction
distinction
desperation
cooperation
alliteration
devastation
hallucination
deception
evolution
resolution
revolution
prescription

Unit 3
possession
obsession
extension
suspension
expansion
corrosion
invasion
exclusion
collision
persuasion
provision
admission
submission
inversion
diversion

Unit 4
flee
pursue
statue
venue
cocoa
mosquito
rodeo
eerie
simile
guarantee
refugee
committee
verandah
debut
alibi

Unit 5
government
parliament
cabinet
politician
minister
senator
representatives
governor
premier
opposition
president
election
democracy
monarchy
federal

Unit 7
synthesise
idiosyncrasy
syndrome
sympathy
symbiotic
symmetry
coherent
cohesive
coincidence
coordinate
accommodate
commotion
compensate
correlate
collaborate

Unit 8
coach
pilot
lifeguard
locksmith
optician
treasurer
choreographer
courier
tutor
sculptor
surgeon
analyst
pharmacist
athlete
paramedic

Unit 9
stability
durability
probability
acceptability
compatibility
predictability
variability
changeability
irritability
visibility
flexibility
vulnerability
accessibility
invincibility
eligibility

Unit 10
environment
rainforest
pollution
greenhouse
climate
recycle
ozone
ecology
irrigation
conservation
deforestation
flora
fauna
sustainable
atmosphere

Unit 11
biology
biography
autobiography
biodegradable
microbe
zoology
zoophobia
anthropology
philanthropy
anthropomorphism
geology
geography
terrace
terrain
terrestrial

Unit 13
prior
senior
superior
exterior
posterior
deteriorate
median
alliance
valiant
pliant
ruffian
peculiar
plagiarise
matriarch
diarrhoea

Unit 14
telescope
periscope
aspect
suspect
auspicious
conspicuous
despise
despicable
spectacle
speculate
sequence
sequel
execute
prosecute
consecutive

Unit 15
wondrous
humorous
perilous
miraculous
Indigenous
cantankerous
studious
gregarious
rebellious
voracious
precarious
instantaneous
spontaneous
righteous
ambiguous

Unit 16
novel
novelty
novice
innovate
innovation
vocal
vocabulary
advocate
vociferous
invoke
provoke
notice
notify
annotate
reminisce

Unit 17
solution
toxic
method
experiment
acid
alkaline
temperature
evaporate
thermometer
theory
equipment
chemical
microscope
hypothesis
laboratory

Unit 19
definit**ion**
repetit**ion**
condemn**ation**
alter**ation**
interpret**ation**
continu**ation**
declar**ation**
cancell**ation**
inflamm**ation**
explan**ation**
exclam**ation**
vari**ation**
identific**ation**
notific**ation**
clarific**ation**

Unit 20
milit**ary**
anivers**ary**
solit**ary**
document**ary**
contr**ary**
crock**ery**
confection**ery**
surg**ery**
nurs**ery**
treach**ery**
forg**ery**
sens**ory**
contradict**ory**
categ**ory**
explorat**ory**

Unit 21
anew
akin
avert
abduct
abhor
abnormal
abolish
abrupt
abuse
adhere
adolescent
adversary
accelerate
accumulate
acquit

Unit 22
symphony
phonetic
microphone
cacophony
synonym
antonym
pseudonym
anonymous
empathy
telepathy
majesty
majority
magnify
magnificent
magnanimous

Unit 23
medicine
bacteria
virus
pregnant
fracture
organ
influenza
abdomen
intestine
capsule
appendix
vaccination
immunisation
pneumonia
stethoscope

Unit 25
cyclone
cynical
cyberspace
urgen**cy**
accura**cy**
litera**cy**
numera**cy**
priva**cy**
pregnan**cy**
diploma**cy**
adequa**cy**
delica**cy**
obstina**cy**
buoyan**cy**
lega**cy**

Unit 26
subconscious
sublime
submerge
subordinate
subside
substandard
subterranean
subtle
succinct
succumb
suffocate
suppose
supplement
surreptitious
suspend

Unit 27
subconscious
sublime
submerge
subordinate
subside
substandard
subterranean
subtle
succinct
succumb
suffocate
suppose
supplement
surreptitious
suspend

Unit 28
incomprehension
unmanageable
discontinued
ignorance
invisibility
irrational
immobile
immovable
noticeably
symmetrical
unintentionally
uncritically
reversible
illegibly
predestined

Unit 29
currency
exchange
pound
euro
rupiah
baht
allowance
financial
budget
discount
subsidy
purchase
expenditure
millionaire
treasury

Unit 31
a**sc**end
de**sc**end
tran**sc**end
ob**sc**ene
adole**scen**t
fluore**scen**t
iride**scen**t
efferve**scen**t
mi**sce**llaneous
su**sce**ptible
convale**sce**
scintillate
con**sci**ence
con**sci**entious
resu**sci**tate

Unit 32
onomatopoeia
asphalt
amateur
havoc
jargon
anemone
flummox
sleuth
nuisance
naive
pizzazz
eclipse
impromptu
labyrinth
conundrum

Unit 33
trek
snorkel
mammoth
deluxe
carnival
rampage
maestro
berserk
gruesome
cologne
abseil
souvenir
gourmet
silhouette
entrepreneur

Unit 34
asteroid
astronaut
astronomy
comet
galaxy
meteor
orbit
dimension
futuristic
chronology
medieval
terrestrial
archaeologist
palaeontology
Renaissance

List words in alphabetical order

abbreviation	Unit 26
abdomen	Unit 23
abduct	Unit 21
abhor	Unit 21
abnormal	Unit 21
abolish	Unit 21
abrupt	Unit 21
abseil	Unit 33
abuse	Unit 21
accelerate	Unit 21
acceptability	Unit 9
accessibility	Unit 9
accommodate	Unit 7
accumulate	Unit 21
accuracy	Unit 25
acid	Unit 17
acquit	Unit 21
adequacy	Unit 25
adhere	Unit 21
adjacent	Unit 1
adjoining	Unit 1
admission	Unit 3
adolescent	Unit 21
adolescent	Unit 31
adversary	Unit 21
advocate	Unit 16
akin	Unit 21
alibi	Unit 4
alkaline	Unit 17
alliance	Unit 13
alliteration	Unit 2
allowance	Unit 29
alteration	Unit 19
amateur	Unit 32
ambiguous	Unit 15
analyst	Unit 8
anemone	Unit 32
anew	Unit 21
anniversary	Unit 20
annotate	Unit 16
anonymous	Unit 22
antonym	Unit 22
appendix	Unit 23
athlete	Unit 8
anthropology	Unit 11
anthropomorphism	Unit 11
apparatus	Unit 26
archaeologist	Unit 34
ascend	Unit 31
aspect	Unit 14
asphalt	Unit 32
assassin	Unit 26
asteroid	Unit 34
astronaut	Unit 34
astronomy	Unit 34
atmosphere	Unit 10
auspicious	Unit 14
autobiography	Unit 11
avert	Unit 21
bacteria	Unit 23
baht	Unit 29
berserk	Unit 33
biodegradable	Unit 11
biography	Unit 11
biology	Unit 11
budget	Unit 29
buoyancy	Unit 25
cabinet	Unit 5
cacophony	Unit 22
cancellation	Unit 19
cantankerous	Unit 15
capsule	Unit 23
carnival	Unit 33
category	Unit 20
changeability	Unit 9
clarification	Unit 19
chemical	Unit 17
choreographer	Unit 8
chronology	Unit 34
climate	Unit 10
coach	Unit 8
cocoa	Unit 4
coherent	Unit 7
cohesive	Unit 7
coincidence	Unit 7
collaborate	Unit 7
collision	Unit 3
cologne	Unit 33
comet	Unit 34
committee	Unit 4
commotion	Unit 7
compatibility	Unit 9
compensate	Unit 7
condemnation	Unit 19
confectionery	Unit 20
contradictory	Unit 20
contrary	Unit 20
conscience	Unit 31
conscientious	Unit 31
consecutive	Unit 14
conservation	Unit 10
conspicuous	Unit 14
continuation	Unit 19
conundrum	Unit 32
convalesce	Unit 31
cooperation	Unit 2
coordinate	Unit 7
correlate	Unit 7
corrosion	Unit 3
corruption	Unit 2
courier	Unit 8
crockery	Unit 20
currency	Unit 29
cyberspace	Unit 25
cyclone	Unit 25
cynical	Unit 25
debut	Unit 4
deception	Unit 2
declaration	Unit 19
definition	Unit 19
deforestation	Unit 10
delicacy	Unit 25
deluxe	Unit 33
democracy	Unit 5
descend	Unit 31
desperation	Unit 2
despicable	Unit 14
despise	Unit 14
deteriorate	Unit 13
devastation	Unit 2
diarrhoea	Unit 13
dilemma	Unit 26
dimension	Unit 34
diplomacy	Unit 25
discontinued	Unit 28
discount	Unit 29
distinction	Unit 2
diversion	Unit 3
documentary	Unit 20
durability	Unit 9
eccentric	Unit 26
eclipse	Unit 32
ecology	Unit 10
eerie	Unit 4
effervescent	Unit 31
election	Unit 5
eligibility	Unit 9
empathy	Unit 22
entrepreneur	Unit 33
environment	Unit 10
equipment	Unit 17
etiquette	Unit 26
euro	Unit 29
evaporate	Unit 17
evolution	Unit 2
exception	Unit 2
exchange	Unit 29
exclamation	Unit 19
exclusion	Unit 3
execute	Unit 14
exhibition	Unit 2
expansion	Unit 3
expenditure	Unit 29
experiment	Unit 17
explanation	Unit 19
exploratory	Unit 20
extension	Unit 3
exterior	Unit 13
fauna	Unit 10
federal	Unit 5
financial	Unit 29
flee	Unit 4
flexibility	Unit 9
flora	Unit 10
flummox	Unit 32
fluorescent	Unit 31
forgery	Unit 20
fracture	Unit 23
futuristic	Unit 34
galaxy	Unit 34
genealogy	Unit 1
genre	Unit 1
geography	Unit 11
geology	Unit 11
geometry	Unit 1
gimmick	Unit 26
gourmet	Unit 33
government	Unit 5
governor	Unit 5
graffiti	Unit 26
greenhouse	Unit 10
gregarious	Unit 15
grudge	Unit 1
gruesome	Unit 33
guarantee	Unit 4
gyrate	Unit 1
hallucination	Unit 2
havoc	Unit 32
hijack	Unit 1
humorous	Unit 15
hypothesis	Unit 17
identification	Unit 19
idiosyncrasy	Unit 7
ignorance	Unit 28
illegibly	Unit 28
immobile	Unit 28
immovable	Unit 28
immunisation	Unit 23
impromptu	Unit 32
incomprehension	Unit 28
Indigenous	Unit 15
indulge	Unit 1
inflammation	Unit 19
influenza	Unit 23
innovate	Unit 16
innovation	Unit 16
instantaneous	Unit 15
intermittent	Unit 26
interpretation	Unit 19
intestine	Unit 23
invasion	Unit 3
inversion	Unit 3
invincibility	Unit 9
invisibility	Unit 28
invoke	Unit 16
iridescent	Unit 31
irrational	Unit 28
irrigation	Unit 10
irritability	Unit 9

SPELLING RULES AND TIPS

The general term for prefixes and suffixes is **affixes**.

Adding ion

If a word ends in **scribe**, change **scribe** to **script** before adding **ion**.

describe → description

If a word ends in **ceive**, change **ceive** to **cept** before adding **ion**.

receive → reception

If a word ends in **t**, change **t** to **ss** before adding **ion**.

admit → admission

If a word ends in **nd**, change **d** to **s** before adding **ion**.

extend → extension

If a word ends in **lve**, change **ve** to **ut** before adding **ion**.

solve → solution

If a word ends in **y**, change the **y** to **i** before adding **cation**.

multiply → multiplication

Some exceptions: *vary → variation* *satisfy → satisfaction*

Adding al

If a noun ends in **ce**, change the **ce** to **ti** before adding **al** to make the adjective.

confidence → confidential

Exceptions: *office → official* *practice → practical*

Adding ity

Words ending in **ible** and **able** are adjectives.
These words may also add **ity** as a second suffix.
Adding **ity** changes the adjective to a noun.

probable → probability *visible → visibility*

The prefix **com-** means *with* or *together*.
Use **com-** before **b**, **p** or **m**. *combine*
Use **col-** before **l**. *collapse*
Use **cor-** before **r**. *correlate*
Use **co-** before **h** or **gn**. *cognition*
Use **con-** in all other cases. *confuse*

The prefix **ad-** means *towards*. Its spelling changes to **ac-** before **c** or **q**.

account *acquit*

The prefix **sub-** means *under* or *less than*. The letter **b** may change to match the beginning consonant of the base word.

submit *suppose* *sufficient* *succumb*

Spelling Rules! Student Book 6 (ISBN 9780655092728) © Janelle Ho, Helen Pearson